ITEM **016 580 166** *17.99*

D1420955

Sonic Boom – Napster, P2P and the
Battle for the Future of Music
John Alderman

SONIC BOOM

SONIC BOOM

NAPSTER, MP3, AND THE NEW PIONEERS OF MUSIC

JOHN ALDERMAN

Foreword by
EVAN I. SCHWARTZ

Preface by
HERBIE HANCOCK

FOURTH ESTATE • *London*

First published in Great Britain in 2001 by
Fourth Estate
A Division of HarperCollins*Publishers*
77–85 Fulham Palace Road
London W6 8JB
www.4thestate.co.uk

A catalogue record for this book is available from the British Library.

ISBN 1-84115-512-8

Printed in Great Britain by
Clays Ltd, St Ives plc

Dedicated to Ernest S. Alderman,
for many years of support.

CONTENTS

Acknowledgements — ix

Foreword by Evan I. Schwartz — xi

Preface by Herbie Hancock — xvii

Introduction — 1

Chapter 1
Wave of Change — 7

Chapter 2
New World Order — 23

Chapter 3
A Culture of Mutation:
The Rising Infrastructure — 33

Chapter 4
Big Breaks and Windfalls — 61

Chapter 5
The Established Order — 81

Chapter 6
A Star Is Born — 101

Chapter 7
No One to Blame — 131

Chapter 8
Out of the Bottle and into Your Ear — 155

Chapter 9
A Pyrrhic Victory? — 169

Notes — 189

Index — 191

ACKNOWLEDGMENTS

I'd like to thank my agent Peter Mcguigan for timely advice and help beyond the call of duty; my editor Jacqueline Murphy for taking a chance and seeing it through; Amanda Cook for the final haul; Gary Wolf and Michael Tanner for initial critiques; Hal Bringman and Phil McGovern for networking assistance; Martha Baer and Kevin Kelleher for believing in the topic back in the early days; Jim Griffin, for his kind words and his Pho mailing list; Herbie Hancock and Evan Schwartz for contributing to this project; and everyone else who gave me their time and perspective. Special words-are-not-enough gratitude go to my wife, Wanida Wannapira, for actually living with me while I wrote a book.

FOREWORD

BY EVAN I. SCHWARTZ

My first epiphany over MP3, Napster, and the like happened in the Bulldog Café, a smoky bar-cum-Internet joint on Amsterdam's Leidesplein. I had deposited six guilders into the machine and was deleting spam and trading dotcom stocks when a young British bloke pulled up next to me. We got to talking about the Net, and the guy, named Darren, told me that he has six gigabytes of music files on his hard drive at home. I was instantly impressed.

Turns out, Darren was a drummer in an indie rock band, and this is how he exposes himself to new music, especially tunes from his favorite band, The Presidents of the United States of America, a Seattle trio that he feels has a particularly amusing song called "Peaches." Just then, his buddy, the guitarist and singer in his band, stepped forward and joined him, harmonizing with their authentic English rock accents: "Moving to the country, gonna eat a lot of peaches. Moving to the country, gonna eat a lot of peaches."

The two also use the Net to distribute and promote their own music. As a result, they have developed a modest following around their hometown in Devon, in the southwest of England, and have used their online status to get gigs, including one playing at the Cavern Club.

"The Cavern Club?" I asked, "Isn't that the place in Hamburg where the Beatles got their start?"

"No, no," said Darren, "The original Cavern Club was in Liverpool. Now we have one near us." The guitarist nodded his head in agreement.

"I thought it was in Hamburg," I said. "Why don't we just look it up online?"

Not sure where to start, I just typed in www.beatles.com. Up came a notice that this site was reserved for future use by Apple Corps, Ltd.

"Wow," I said. "That's interesting."

"Apple?" said Darren. "What does a computer company have to do with the Beatles?" The guitarist had a similarly puzzled expression.

"You guys can't be serious," I said. "You're musicians from England, and you don't know the relationship between Apple and the Beatles?"

Now, I'm not one of those 1960s guys. I was swishing around in a uterus somewhere when the Beatles played Ed Sullivan. But I am old enough to have spent a part of my youth watching apples spinning around turntables while memorizing the lyrics to Sgt. Pepper's. Even my Beatle CDs have the little Apple logo on it. But then it struck me: Not only have these guys never probably owned an album, but they probably don't even think in terms of CDs or albums. Songs to them are listed on screens, then downloaded and played. It was different than what I was used to. And when I ran this theory by them, they agreed that while they are keenly interested in music, they weren't much interested in knowing which song was on which album or about record labels at all. They had a new way of thinking about music.

This, to me, was an even bigger revelation than the news nearly a year earlier that one of my favorite bands in the world, They Might Be Giants, would post MP3 files on Yahoo and thus become the first major label band to offer a new album for initial release on the Internet. Like everyone else, my question was: How are they going to make money from this?

But since then, I've concluded that such artists are probably going to gain more from these new online and wireless formats than they will lose due to so-called copyright infringement. Listening to the new TMBG songs only made me want to go see the band play those songs.

Then it occurred to me that what is just as valuable as copyright—if not more so—is an artist's trademark. They Might Be Giants was savvy enough to file for a trademark on their name, protecting the identity of their performance services, way back in 1990, around the time of their classic CD release, *Flood*. The Beatles, by contrast, didn't have their first U.S. trademark registered until 1993. (It was filed, incidentally, by Apple Corps, Ltd.) Anyone can check whether favorite artists have filed for trademarks, simply by searching the official trademark database at www.uspto.gov.

My point is this: Artists who grumble about copyright infringement but fail to trademark their own names don't know the value of their own work.

If you want to understand the rising importance of trademarks and the sinking importance of copyright, just talk to William R. Bradley, a partner with Glankler Brown, the Memphis law firm that represents Elvis Presley Enterprises, Inc., which was created by the late singer's estate to make money from his intellectual property. "The Net poses a real challenge to copyright," Bradley says. "The rights to protect against unauthorized reproduction are simply too hard to enforce. You'll be chasing everybody."

To better protect and serve Elvis, the estate in recent years has been on a trademark tear. It first trademarked the name Elvis Presley and his Graceland mansion in the mid-1980s. Then the company moved to trademark Elvis's hit songs, even though Elvis didn't actually write any of them. In the mid-1990s, the company trademarked "Heartbreak Hotel" for a licensed restaurant chain, then for use on pants, shorts, shirts, sweatshirts, jackets, hats, and socks, and then on shot glasses, martini glasses, goblets, and tumblers. Turns out, there is money to be made in such officially licensed stuff.

So now, the estate is moving to trademark "All Shook Up" for use on key chains, cigarette lighters, Christmas tree ornaments, float pens, and snow globes. Also in the works are "Love Me Tender" spoons, bumper stickers, and golf balls, as well as trademarks for merchandise bearing the marks "Don't Be Cruel," "Hound Dog," "Jailhouse Rock," and of course "Blue Suede Shoes," which alas may eventually be used to brand everything except navy leather footwear.

All this has symbolic significance because copyright law affords no protection whatsoever to song titles, album titles, book titles, or movie titles. Remember, a copyright simply protects a unique expression. I can release an album tomorrow called *Sgt. Pepper's Lonely Hearts Club Band*. I can market a movie called *Gone with the Wind*. I can publish a book called *Harry Potter*. And I can record a song called "Margaritaville." As long as I'm not copying someone else's unique expression, no one can stop me. However, if I wanted to make Sgt. Pepper's cocktail sauce, *Gone with the Wind* foot powder, a Harry Potter magic wand, or "Margaritaville" brand tequila, I may encounter some serious legal turbulence.

More importantly, if I wanted to advertise my performance services—give a Harry Potter reading or a Sgt. Pepper's concert—I'd probably also encounter some legal roadblocks. This is how trademarks can work to protect copyrights and extract additional value from them. And this is why trademarks are so important to artists, writers, musicians, and other producers of intellectual property, even though most are only now coming to realize this. *Sgt. Pepper's* was never trademarked by the Beatles, but *Harry Potter* is vigorously trademarked in several categories of goods and services. And Jimmy Buffett is already kicking back and collecting royalties from officially licensed tequila. Nowadays, trademarks are simply much easier to enforce than are copyrights.

Once you begin to feel the power of trademarks, you'll see that something like Napster can actually help generate income. If you're an artist whose intellectual property is being swapped around for free online, then every download can potentially enhance the awareness of your trademarks, including your name and the titles of your works. This is precisely why so many unestablished artists are fully supportive of Napster. They know that any increased awareness of their songs might lead to interest not only in purchasing their CDs but in their trademarked performance services, their brand.

A former Grateful Dead lyricist, John Perry Barlow, likes to say that intellectual property is a misnomer, that it's not really property at all, but should be thought of more as an intellectual *relationship* between the artist and the audience. As a writer, I don't think I'd go so far as to renounce all of my property rights. But I do believe strongly in the relationship thing. And I believe the two can coexist.

And so John Alderman's book couldn't have arrived at a better time. In addition to being a great story in itself, *Sonic Boom* details the new rebellion in rock, defines the raging conflicts posed by new technology, and points the way toward striking a new balance between property and relationships. Hopefully, established artists will be able to adapt to this new music environment. The up-and-coming ones already seem to be well on their way. Those blokes from Devon, wherever they may be right now, are recording and have already played at their local Cavern Club. Maybe they'll even make it to the original one—in Liverpool.

PREFACE

BY HERBIE HANCOCK

I'm deeply concerned about the outcome of the online music conflict, and with good reason: playing music happens to be my livelihood. Now the Internet comes along and offers not only wonderful promise and incredibly seductive dangers, but it also is helping to inflame long-running conflicts within the current music distribution system. *Sonic Boom* documents both the possibilities and the pitfalls, as it points to the tough choices facing all sides of online music players. Like others in my profession, I make the best music I can, drawing from experience, years of practice, and plenty of dues paid. In return, audiences seek out and listen to my recordings or attend live performances, mostly paying for the privilege. In the middle of that relationship stands the record company, hopefully making sure that listeners get a chance to hear me, so that I am able to continue my career doing what I love.

For the hard work involved in being a middleman, the label is certainly entitled to a decent profit. But not a killing. To make huge amounts of money on the backs of artists who are not fairly compensated sours the relationship and creates bad will that lasts a long time. Believe me, I'm not happy about the business model that the record companies have been running until now. They have proven again and again that they are far from angels, far from having even a casual interest in giving artists and songwriters a fair share. They have been ripping off artists, writers, and the public for close to a century, to the point where I can honestly say I don't trust them at all. Knowing what they do about past bad faith makes artists bristle when the industry says it's just trying to "defend artists' rights." Who wouldn't resent being used as a pawn this way?

Napster, on the other hand, is no solution. So far, it's even worse than the labels. On the way to making millions for its owners and investors, Napster has yet to give anything to artists other than the chance to spread their music, for free, and whether they like it or not. Its supporters hide behind claims that labels misuse artists and consumers, as if that entitled them to take everything they want absolutely free. *Excuse me, but* just because record executives give artists a bad deal doesn't mean that everyone else can then go and do worse. Although the appeal to consumers is obvious—who wouldn't want free music?—the law, and common morality, forbids stealing. I'm not afraid of technology, and I hope that a system can be worked out that enables consumers that would also reward artists. Maybe this is even the beginning of what might grow into something great. I'm still a little worried. Looking at the past behavior on either side of *RIAA vs. Napster* makes it hard to get behind any new industry plans for the future.

I understand that the RIAA's idea is to shut Napster down, or force them into legitimate business deals, such as Bertelsmann has proposed. What I'd like to know is what these deals will mean for musicians, singers, and songwriters—the people without whom there would be nothing to fight over, nothing for these multinational companies to make money from, and nothing for music lovers to enjoy. I'd feel like a fool if Napster were shut down or forced into a deal, and the courts gave millions to the record companies but the artists received zilch.

If the RIAA gets some kind of injunction or other legal action supported by the courts that will allow the artists and writers to have a choice regarding how their music is distributed on the Net, then that is a great and positive step. If there is a great deal of money to go to the record companies and the RIAA has no idea how those labels will compensate artists, then a big gaping hole is left to fester. Who represents artists in this picture? So far, it seems like no one.

INTRODUCTION

The advent of the Internet has been a relentless series of wrenching headaches and embarrassing mistakes for the music industry. It has also allowed unprecedented worldwide distribution of music and unparalleled communication among fans and musicians—unambiguous blessings for music itself. But such success is still set against the backdrop of an industry struggling to maintain control and remain relevant. Over the greater part of the last century, the entities that would come to be the big five record labels—Warner, Universal, BMG, Sony, and EMI—crafted elaborate distribution pipelines to generate and safeguard hefty revenue by combining street smarts, cultural savvy, tough-guy tricks, and crafty legal maneuvering with keenly developed business sense. It's only recently that they were settling into the more regular life of multinational corporations. Now these companies and a few others confront the greatest challenge of their history. They find themselves in an environment in which their chief commodity is not just easily converted into digital code—ripe for limitless copying and dissemination—but also is spread via a worldwide network that dwarfs anything that came before it. While innovators speculate about the benefits to human progress a free-flowing pipeline of information brings, the music industry has plenty of reservations: It was banking on its control of songs that have now become seductive little packets of freely traded digits.

1

Visit a college campus almost anywhere in America, and you're sure to find two things: computer networks with high-speed, high-bandwidth Internet connections, and music fans who have amassed large collections of music without ever buying tapes, CDs, or records. Instead of trips to the record store, many simply download the songs they want from a school network, or hook up with fans elsewhere, trading songs with Napster or its many clones. Go to a record company in Manhattan or Los Angeles, and you're likely to find two things: executives with great resistance to technological change and someone in the IT department who avidly follows online developments and may have even accumulated a collection of MP3s. This situation seems so pervasive that it has replaced the old stereotype of the A&R staff asking the mailroom clerk for tips about which new bands are hip.

The big-record-label–dominated music business that developed in the last century is now under assault by successive waves of young techies such as Napster's Shawn Fanning and Gnutella creator Justin Frankel and their tsunami of followers. These arbiters of innovation share several traits, namely technical ingenuity and priorities that fall polar opposite to traditional business. A half decade ago, when the Web was in its infancy, it was popular to say that programmers were the new rock stars. Despite a few renegade cyberpunk coders sporting leather pants and mirrored sunglasses, the notion quickly faded as the reality of a high-tech workforce became more mundane. But looking at the innovation and bravado of the young people who have brought such a dramatic crisis to the music business, it's easy to see some truth in the old statement, particularly when these visionaries are contrasted with the current crop of top-selling artists. The challenge to the old guard that the young coders present seems more fundamentally unsettling than most rock and roll these days, and their rebellion seems more genuine and more compelling than the packaged and exaggerated posing of record industry poster boys.

Technology brings power, and the level of technology now in the hands of individuals will present challenges to everyone with a vested interest in the status quo. In response to those challenges, government and corporations may overstep acceptable boundaries and seek to infringe on the rights of individuals whose protections as citizens should come before their roles as consumers. Music distribution on the Internet is interesting because it is showing, to anyone paying attention, how things might progress in many other industries, particularly those with a product that can be digitized. That the MP3 format is a subset of a standard meant for the compression of movies is a glaring clue as to the next big industry likely to be touched by the mercurial hand of the Net.

The music industry has a long history of legal skirmishes with the inventors and builders of new music players. The audiocassette and digital audio tape (DAT) are two recent examples that seemed to work out advantageously for the music business. In the 1980s, when cassette tapes were the latest threat to copyright holders, legislators granted music labels a portion of every sale of blank tapes. The industry later that same decade worked to kill DAT as a consumer format with threats of lawsuits. Digital tape was able to record at higher fidelity than CDs and wouldn't degrade with each generation, so it was feared as the perfect medium for bootlegging. But because of high cost resulting from fewer machines, demand for DAT never spread much beyond dedicated concert tapers and musicians.

With the right software, personal computers are now able to do anything that DAT players can, and they have proven very hard to regulate. Software and hardware makers have the economic and growing political power to compete with the music industry, so they've been able to stave off most of the industry's legal assaults. But when the makers of new technologies are only sometimes corporations—and are often just a kid in a dorm—the equation changes remarkably. Because new players, and new methods of distributing what's played, exist as code, manufacturing and retailing are unneeded. That leaves ample room to innovate without some of the traditional business, financial, and legal obstacles (and without their protections). A good new product, especially if the creator is not so interested in remuneration, could be released in one day, and by the next week there might be a million copies in circulation worldwide. The MP3 world is filled with software that has been distributed in such a way. On the music side, legally or not, a popular song follows the same lightning path. Bootlegged songs from Radiohead's *Kid A* were downloaded by millions of Net users before the album was officially released. Smashing Pumpkins broke with its label, Virgin, and gave away the group's final album for free distribution on the Net. It met a similarly massive response.

The groundbreaking ability of people across the planet to freely share information is changing the world and our culture, and this presents a scary prospect for those hoping to make money in exchange for the time and resources invested in producing and marketing to that culture. If a band and its producer are accustomed to spending a year and several hundred thousand dollars recording and touring to promote a record, it's easy to see how they might fear the new ability of anyone to send a copy of whatever they like, for free. Unlike illusionary changes in styles and personae, or even corporate acquisitions and mergers, this fundamental shift changes even the form that music takes. Digital distribution means that music is no longer tied to an object such as a record, tape, or CD, but becomes, as it is being shared and consumed, something more ethereal. Depending on how you look at it, in the online world, music has been either stripped or liberated from its body; only its soul remains, its digital code. If a record company has spent millions to develop and control the works of musicians, banking on their value as consumer goods—marketable, singular objects—company officials might be shocked to discover what they hope to sell and control has become pure information, flowing freely around the globe.

While the record companies and the Recording Industry Association of America (RIAA) dominate media reports and courtroom dramas, musicians themselves have been polarized by online music. Metallica's Lars Ulrich raged against online traders. But archly antiestablishment bands like the English Chumbawamba have seized the moment to air long-standing grievances: Despite their high-minded talk, most record companies "wouldn't recognise art or artistic integrity if it bounded over and bit them on the arse," Chumbawamba vocalist Dunstan Bruce said on his band's Web site. "The real truth is that record companies have been screwing the public for years and they're now terrified that they might lose the odd dollar here and there." Nor is it simply the outsiders or the more usual publicity seekers like Courtney Love who have found something to say. Elton John struck a tone similar to Love's anger at the industry at a press conference. The Who's Pete Townshend (also using his own Web site to send a message) wrote that the first thing that struck him when he went online with Napster and found "such a lot of stuff" when he searched on his name was "hooray—at last I might as well say fuck BMI."

If it looked as if the labels were paralyzed by a financial interest in the status quo and were ignoring a larger, developing picture, other businessmen followed the money to seek common ground with Napster, the most feared, most popular of the online predators. Just as urgently as most music industry executives sought to kill their online adversaries, or at least subdue them as they did the cassette tape, other business leaders were stalking something much bigger. For a mere $50 million, the same amount he invested in 1994 when he struck gold with a budding AOL, Bertelsmann's Thomas Middelhoff helped out an embattled Napster, hoping to buy into the future. Going over the head of its music division to cut a deal with the global Napster phenomenon, can Bertelsmann find a way to make the new world work for the suits as well as the pirates? As youngsters come home from college infecting their families with the joy of instant, unfiltered access to all the songs they can remember, turning back the clock not only becomes virtually impossible, taking away the music sounds to almost everyone like a really bad idea. This book is about the battle for that cultural soul that is being fought by college students, entrepreneurs, lawyers, moguls, programmers, and of course, by musicians themselves.

WAVE OF CHANGE

On the sunny afternoon of May 3, 2000, a mixed crowd of techies, music fans, and reporters began to assemble in front of an uninspiring beige building on a street corner in San Mateo, California. The city, one of several businesslike and nearly identical adjacent burgs, was set in the middle of the giant, remarkably expensive sprawl of asphalt, hills, and vegetation stretching from wind-chilled San Francisco in the north to the warmer Silicon Valley in the south. Gathering demonstrators, mostly white, middle class, and in their twenties or thirties, locked their cars outside of the well-tended apartment buildings that lined the street. Parking, the last-minute foil to many would-be demonstrations, was easily found, and the gathered forces seemed to be in good spirits, striking up amiable chats as they walked towards the excitement. A visitor might be struck with the reality of many California stereotypes playing themselves out. It was warm with a pleasant breeze, flowering plants and trees spread a soothing fragrance, and it was difficult to erase the feeling that this street was an interchangeable set; even the protest felt oddly ready-made, like the anonymous blocks that passed for a downtown nearby.

It was one of those moments that felt like an intermission, when personalities and social forces came together in the flesh, outside of the more controlled and familiar media where most people had come to know them.

Though the atmosphere grew increasingly frenetic as one approached the Napster offices, the mood of the attendees was mostly one of curiosity livened with the anticipation of spectacle. A few police cars stopped mid-street without pulling over; other vehicles slowed down as lunching office workers rubbernecked, and occasionally someone honked and shook his fist out the window, or displayed another gesture of support—though it was often unclear what was being supported. More than anything else, the air that day was full of mixed feelings. Metallica, one of the most respected and top-selling heavy metal bands of the 1980s and '90s, was about to deliver a challenge to the spirit of manifest destiny that often seemed ingrained in the technologically savvy. Drummer Lars Ulrich and the band's attorneys were about to drop off a list of over 300,000 names, taking Napster at its word that it would deny service to those who'd been spotted trading unauthorized songs.

The largest contingent of spectators that day were from the media, and by far the greatest animosity on display was from photographers jostling for good position, or reporters swarming around the few participants who actually started to say something. Five or so Napster supporters held up a long banner denouncing Metallica and the Recording Industry Association of America as "Master of Puppets," the title of one of the band's songs. Reps from other online music companies circled around the building in cars, slowing down to hand off their own branded freebies to an eager, antsy audience. Two young men who worked at a calendar publisher's office in the same building as Napster had taken opposite sides of the debate and explained their positions to the gathered reporters who attentively jotted down their every pronouncement; for them it seemed great to take a break from routine, nice to have their opinions taken seriously. One explained that sharing music, even for free, helped artists in the long run by making them famous; the other insisted that Metallica alone had the right to decide what happened to its music. A musician named Marc Brown was quoted by the Associated Press as saying, "I have sympathy in the sense that if a ton of money was at stake for me, I might act like this also. But, objectively, I don't think that they deserve any sympathy."

Soon a large black SUV pulled up, and while the crowd moved closer, Lars Ulrich and Howard King, his burly lawyer, stepped out and pushed through to the building. An associate wheeled a trolley containing a brown cardboard box, filled with reams of paper, the list of 335,435 names. Surrounded by a crowd near the entrance to the building, Ulrich turned and read a speech that was a rehash of statements he'd been making through his PR agents, about how Metallica didn't approve of anyone trading Internet files of their music, and how Napster itself was responsible for theft. To the dismay of fame seekers, the midday glare diminished much of Ulrich's glamour, and having a mass of lawyers around him didn't look too rock and roll. He was only beginning what would become a personal crusade and was still a little fuzzy on some of the details. But, believing his band, and many others, were being wronged by the culture of trading that was so rapidly growing, he was determined to do his best to point out the injustice. The embodiment of rebel angst was having trouble shifting gears to righteous do-gooder, though. When asked about the consequences of his coming out as a spokesman for an industry perceived as being "the man," Ulrich switched quickly from wounded artist to his more familiar role as devil-may-care rebel. "Metallica doesn't give a fuck about anything. If it looks right for us we just go for it; we don't worry about the consequences."

Ulrich then turned and entered the building, his entourage and the cardboard box in tow, and went upstairs to an office described by other visitors as neatly segregated between young and old workers. He met with Napster representatives for about ten minutes. Ulrich's mood seemed to lighten somewhat by the time he came out. He said that the sides "agreed to disagree" and appeared relieved that "there are actual humans inside." The Metallica team sped away, and the remaining gawkers stood around aimlessly for a few quiet moments, as reporters rushed off to deliver their stories. Thus began Ulrich's publicity campaign, which would be followed by online chats on Yahoo, by an interview with TV's Charlie Rose, in counterpoint to Public Enemy's Chuck D, and by a speech before a congressional hearing. Ulrich would be cheered and maligned, a visible target for the industry and fans.

Napster spokespersons dismissed the Metallica provocation as a "publicity stunt," but agreed to suspend the service of the 335,435 users, who were identified by NetPD, a British consulting firm. "Of course," said a Napster attorney, Laurence Pulgram, "if the band would provide the names in computerized form, rather than in tens of thousands of pages of paper intended to create a photo op, that would expedite the process."

By all reports, Napster's founder, Shawn Fanning, was ruffled at being the focus of negative attention from one of his heroes. "I'm a huge Metallica fan and therefore really sorry that they're going in this direction," said Fanning, in a statement. "Napster respects the role of artists and is very interested in working with Metallica and the music industry to develop a workable model that is fair to everyone while unleashing the power of the Internet to build enthusiasm for music." From that moment forward, Fanning would appear frequently dressed in a Metallica T-shirt, most famously as a presenter at the MTV Music Awards, where Ulrich sat in the audience looking sick. It was difficult to say whether the *Beavis and Butthead*–like fashion statement was meant to be mocking or merely the honest expression of a fan laced with a little irony. Whatever the case, Ulrich made clear that, as far as he was concerned, being a Napster user and a Metallica fan were incompatible: on television and the Internet, he directly told fans who used Napster that the band didn't want their types.

Like Metallica, everyone in music and the Internet seemed busy going for whatever they thought to be in their immediate interest, and they didn't seem worried about the consequences. Heavy penalties loomed, like the threats of multimillion dollar entertainment business lawsuits. But the long arm of the law did little to stop the relentless boasts of computer whiz kids who believed that copyright would soon be rendered meaningless. And this was the public dialogue. On private mailing lists, the threats by either side were more graphic and more personal, including death threats, meant however jokingly. No one needed a reminder that the coming year would see more bile than ever.

How did the development of new technologies that supported a *leisure time* activity such as music reach this level of venom? And was all the confrontation—and all the lawyers—really necessary? Probably not. But because both computer developers and music industry lawyers had a history of getting what they wanted, the legal force and the adolescent aggression seemed inevitable.

*   *   *

The sleepy, beachside city of Santa Cruz, California, is known for several things: a good university with a reputation for intellectual adventure; a population of New-Agey free spirits; and a natural environment that seems to infuse a mellow hedonism in most of its inhabitants. While very typically Californian, the city feels like the polar opposite of Los Angeles: little crime, no frantic social climbing, and certainly not much in the way of an entertainment industry. In 1993, at least in as much as any event on the Web can be said to occur in one place, Santa Cruz became the birthplace of the online music phenomenon.

The wave of change that would see fans turning to the Internet for their tunes, and away from the distribution networks built by large entertainment corporations, began, as is so often the case, with a couple of bright collegiate misfits. Though they did very little research, not much coding, and developed no new ways to compress music, what they did was build a Web site that offered a new way for people to get music and for musicians to reach an audience.

The buzzing of Web activity gave the West Coast a portentous feeling that year. Nationally, the time was ripe for invention. While the Reagan era sometimes felt like a long backward glance, Bill Clinton and Al Gore had just begun an administration that at the very least embraced an optimistic, forward-looking vocabulary, spotlighting initiatives that pushed the new "information superhighway." In the business world, offices that had never before even needed calculators were suddenly acquiring computers that sprawled over desktops to become the focus of a worker's attention. News of the Internet was beginning to pique the interest of the public and the media. *Wired* magazine had launched its first issue, including an article about libraries replacing their books with digitized copies, an idea with obvious overlap in other media. The story wondered, "if someday in the future anybody can get an electronic copy of any book from a library free of charge, why should anyone ever set foot in a bookstore again?" The focus on print was predictable; text was much easier to send over low bandwidth, and the Net was built largely around words. Meanwhile, those with an interest in music were wondering what the Internet could do for them. About the same time *Wired* was launched, a pair of University of California Santa Cruz students hatched a plan to answer that question.

The pair doing the hatching were Jeff Patterson and Rob Lord, two friends who shared a love for music, as well as a distaste for the bland offerings of mainstream record labels. Patterson was a lanky, long-haired blond; Lord, olive-skinned and often seen wearing an amused, knowing smile. Before going away to school, Lord had been manager of a record store in his hometown of Valencia, California. Being the final link in the long chain of the music business was an experience that shaped his feeling towards the establishment. The narrow range of available product and the heavy-handed marketing of the industry put him off. His own preferences leaned towards college radio staples like the anguished cries of Joy Division or the lush and dreamy washes of sound made by Galaxy 500, as well as music from the burgeoning rave scene—distant cries from the mass-market records he usually sold.

"I was the stereotypical music store employee," explained Lord, "saying things like 'Barbra Streisand—you can't listen to her, and you can't kill her . . . Beep.' Like any discerning music fan, you ended up selling all of this music that you wished people wouldn't buy. I kept thinking to myself that if only there were a better way of getting better music distribution."

Patterson was equally frustrated with the narrow range of musical choices readily available and was miffed by the few options open to musicians wanting to expose their works to a wider audience. He had firsthand experience in that regard and was hoping there might be a way for his band, The Ugly Mugs, to expose its music—songs with names like "Cold Turd on a Paper Plate"—to people who would appreciate it. Music like his wouldn't be released by Warner or BMG, but would probably appeal to a larger audience than Santa Cruz slackers, if only the songs could get out there.

At school, Lord studied information theory and digital signal processing, fortuitously under the tutelage of David Huffman, whose Huffman encoding algorithm was popularly in use (it was, as it happened, a main component of the MP3 protocols). Lord also worked part-time as the computer consultant to the UC art department. His encounter with the newly developing Web was deeply affecting and he became gripped with a fervor to promulgate Web browsers to anyone within reach. Mosaic was the most popular browser available at the time. Freshly released by the National Center for Supercomputing Applications, it featured a graphic user interface that made using it easy. Lord diligently installed copies of Mosaic on all of the department's computers. The idea of a universal interface to data, combined with new audio compression and player technologies he was learning about under Huffman, sparked an epiphany in Lord, and he and Patterson began to brainstorm ideas about how to combine the two. A decent student, Lord was nonetheless not thrilled with school; he claims he wasn't having enough fun and was hoping to find something that might combine his two passions: music and technology. That something would materialize one day as Lord trolled the Internet, searching for interesting ways to compress sound files (compressing the data in a music file was necessary to send it manageably over the Internet). He discovered the Xing Player, a piece of software that played musical files compressed using the MP2 algorithm. A quick download and a listen was all it took to hook Lord, and his life took a quick, profound turn. He became a cheerleader, what could even be called an evangelist, for online music. His e-mail signature line read "Free or Shareware Music,

Internet Distribution of Music Will Change All," with a link pointing everyone towards the Xing Player. Friends and acquaintances followed his suggestion, and years before Napster hit, Lord became a key figure in a clique that seemed to instinctively understand the power that Internet distribution held for music.

With ambitions to bring together as much music-related content as he could get his hands on, Lord opened an account at the popular public server Sunsite, which let him store his Web site for anyone to download. From there, inspired by revolutionary dreams and technological fervor, Lord and Patterson took the leap to launch one of the Web's first start-up companies. Internet Underground Music Archive, or IUMA, was set up in a small office above a Santa Cruz gay bar. The Web start-up pattern was in full effect from day one: Lord and Patterson slept under their desks, and paid the wages of the few acting school dropouts they'd managed to recruit as employees by picking up a weekly burrito tab.

At first, IUMA was really two sites in one, one on the Web, which required greater computing power than many had in that day, and one that used "File Transfer Protocol" or FTP. The sites gave bands a place to tell the world about themselves and also to offer music for download. Much of the music IUMA hosted was initially sent in on cassette tape, leaving the encoding to the staff, for which the company charged a small fee. Anyone could pay $240 a year and post one song and band photos and offer merchandise for sale. It was a learning experience for all involved. It gave Lord, among other things, a lesson in the power of PR. Following the other now-familiar Web start-up pattern, the media was quick to pick up on IUMA's high-tech buzz, and the newly minted executive quickly learned to fan the fires of publicity with revolutionary rhetoric.

"This is going to kill the music industry," Lord proclaimed to the *San Jose Mercury News* in 1993. From the pages of the Silicon Valley daily newspaper, it was a quick jump to CNN and then the cover of *Billboard*. The music industry had a new and boisterous, if somewhat ill-defined and as yet naïve, foil. Like a clever youngster testing limits, Lord and IUMA helped point the Internet generation at a new target against which it could gauge its growing strength. The music industry was a dinosaur that didn't understand the promise of the Net and had stifled its own creativity through the pursuit of corporate profits. This unsteady new establishment wanted to take over.

IUMA promised to be the place where less overtly commercial bands could create Web pages and reach more diverse audiences, despite the high-tech threshold for Internet use. In 1993, less than 3 percent of American classrooms were connected to the Net, compared to more than half in 2000. Even when traffic was minimal, music clips were being downloaded from as far away as Russia—an appealing prospect to bands unaccustomed to being heard outside their hometowns. Remember, at the time it was novel to make human contact of any kind using your computer; to have distant foreigners visit your Web site and listen to music you had just kicked out seemed very futuristic indeed. As the country, and the stock market, became obsessed with Internet technology, the pace picked up, and the breadth and speed of Internet delivery accelerated. In a 1994 issue of early cyber-culture magazine *Mondo 2000*, avant-garde musician Kenneth Newby interviewed Lord and Patterson and described IUMA as a "kind of digital club where the bands play for free, there's no cover charge, and the owners are just happy that you came."

This kind of description echoed popular expectations of the Web in general, raising a question that would haunt nearly everyone who had some creative, digitized product that they hoped to sell on the Web: How did the Internet develop into a giant playground where everyone expected things to be free? Once a piece of work was digitized, Web users seemed to instinctively feel that it was fair game for anyone who wanted to download it.

The recording industry seemed unconcerned with IUMA, and if it noticed at all, it was to take advantage of IUMA's service, on a very small scale. The small, progressive, Warner-affiliated label 4AD Records, for example, had Web pages created for its bands. Other than that, music industry insiders simply made a note to have a talk with IUMA's founders, to affirm that they were all interested in doing cool stuff.

As Harvard professor Lawrence Lessig has put it, the code from which the Net is built is the law. Many of the expectations about on-line music are the legacy of builders themselves, and many beliefs are based on the structure of the networks. Those who built the Web, though a very diverse bunch, tended to share many similar goals. The Internet, of course, arose from the bowels of the Cold War infrastructure of military and education. It was a way of distributing research and military data using computer networks that spurted "packets" of information across multiple lines to be later reassembled into their original form at the final destination. The system, as developed at the U.S. Advanced Research Projects Agency (ARPA), promised a quick, if somewhat quirky method of communication that included not only the sharing of programs and data over great distance, but also radio messaging that would not break down due to jamming or geography.

For a research-oriented group, the ability to share data from around the country and around the world was the main interest. The likelihood of commercial rights holders asserting their claims was not much of a concern; in fact all commercial activity was officially off-limits on the Net until 1991. Commercial interest wasn't great anyway until the World Wide Web transformed the rather arcane communication tools of the Net into lively multimedia portals, ready to open on command on the screens of the workforce, student body, and swelling ranks of home users who were just getting comfortable with their PCs.

Many of those involved in the creation of the Web had lofty, socially ambitious goals that involved making it as easy as possible to share information, and many expected to foster a leap in human knowledge and culture that could usher in another Renaissance. "The Web," Tim Berners-Lee wrote, "was designed as an instrument to prevent misunderstandings." The system that he designed encouraged the free spread of what would later be called "content," and he was not alone in feeling inspired by beliefs that were strongly optimistic, even verging on utopian.

"The whole spread of the Web happened not because of a decision and a mandate from any specific authority, but because a whole bunch of people across the 'Net picked it up and brought up Web clients and servers," Berners-Lee wrote in an essay about the overlapping goals of the Web and Unitarian religion. "The actual explosion of creativity, and the coming into being of the Web was the result of thousands of individuals playing a small part. In the first couple of years, often this was not for a direct financial gain, but because they had an inkling that it was the right way to go, and a gleam of an exciting future."

The Web was at first slow and buggy, especially for home users, but the excitement of a multimedia network was catchy, and what can only be described as a mass migration of work and culture online began. Because the impact of the Web was so profound and widespread, many metaphors were tossed around in an attempt to describe and assess its impact. Comparisons to Gutenberg's development of the printing press, highways, and casbahs all reflected the particular viewpoints of the describers, most of whom were in awe of the potential. After all, a lot had been done with tools as simple as e-mail, mailing lists, and bulletin boards. It was just those kinds of tools, together with the tape recorder, that had been the secret behind the success of the Grateful Dead.

The first online mailing list ever dedicated to a single group (originating at the Stanford Artificial Intelligence Lab) was dedicated to the Dead. "It was appropriate that it was about the Grateful Dead," explained Steve Silberman, probably the most articulate expert on the band, "because the Grateful Dead was one of the first groups to develop a truly mobile community of fans, who would follow the band from venue to venue on every tour. The way that the Dead played music was inextricably related to the fact that they developed a mobile community of fans."

Silberman believed that the experiences of the band and its fans carry insight about the nature of musical communities when they meet the power of electronic networking. The Grateful Dead changed their set lists every night, and they changed the way they played each song every night. That *modus operandi* inspired Stanley Owsley, an LSD chemist and visionary sound engineer, to suggest to the band, sometime around 1968, that they should record every show to amass a vault of recordings.

As the band began recording live performances, fans followed suit with their own recordings. The Dead gave a free concert on Haight Street in San Francisco in 1968, and a reel-to-reel tape of that show was recorded by one Steve Brown. That tape ended up being copied and passed around by soldiers in Vietnam, after Brown took it with him when he went over for a tour of duty. It became a "coveted" item among the Deadheads who were fighting, said Silberman, who has written an encyclopedia on The Dead, *Skeleton Key*.

As the network of traders grew, they initially relied on exchanging business cards at shows to stay in touch. Then, as the personal computer surged in popularity, Deadheads were among the largest cultural groups of early adopters, mostly due to the incredible usefulness of bulletin board systems or BBSs, dial-in computer networks that not only let you trade gossip and tapes, but also let you make friends with—and stay in daily contact with—members of the Dead inner circle. At the top of the BBS list was famed California electronic community the WELL, started by Stewart Brand, the *Whole Earth Catalog* publisher and Merry Prankster. Being on the WELL gave you a huge logistical advantage if you were a Deadhead in the late '80s and early '90s, said Silberman, because it allowed privileged access to those who could secure coveted tickets and make early announcements about tour dates. The WELL also offered Internet access, so that fans could use some online repositories that had begun to sprout up.

"Even before MP3s became big there were people who were creating FTP directories with everything from digitized photos and art, to set lists, to the entire career of the band in electronic form, complete with electronic documents," Silberman explained. "Now there are these very deep directories that are passed secretly by e-mail, where 500 Dead shows have been digitized, either song by song or set by set." The addresses to these treasure troves are closely guarded, for fear of being swamped by downloaders and overloading the servers.

"The interesting thing about Garcia saying 'When we're through with [the music], it's theirs' was that it created this model for building the value of intellectual property by giving it away," Silberman said.

By letting fans do whatever they wanted with taped concert music, the Dead made their music more valuable because people wanted more of it, and furthermore, they wanted to be there when that magic was being made: "The tapes cast an event quality over what would otherwise be perceived as just another show. Each tape was as good as an album, so it was like being invited to hear a new album being created 150 nights a year. What really created the Deadhead community was the ability to trade tapes, and once the online world came around, it was the perfect way to do it."

Flash forward to the late '90s and things were not looking so rosy for the Dead. After Jerry Garcia died (and became one of the first celebrities to receive a spontaneous wave of scores of personal and private Web pages offered in memorial), the band's income was sharply cut. "They're in a very difficult position now, because they were an animal that was kept alive by touring," said Silberman. "When Jerry died, the touring income went from enough to make them one of the top-grossing bands in America, to very little, because the Phil and Friends shows and the other shows turned out not to be as much of a draw. They laid everybody off." At the beginning of 2001, there were fewer than a dozen people in the Dead office, down from sixty or so.

Another legacy that the Grateful Dead community contributed to the online world was their lyricist, John Perry Barlow. Barlow, a former Wyoming rancher and sometime mentor of John F. Kennedy, Jr., was one of the more outspoken figures on the media and lecture circuit that developed around the Internet early in the '90s. In 1990 Barlow cofounded a nonprofit Internet advocacy group called the Electronic Frontier Foundation to combat the enacting of what he considered unfair and uninformed laws to regulate the Internet. Although Barlow's self-promotion and mildly affected cowboy/hippie/ladies' man persona earned him some rolled eyes wherever he spoke, audiences soon found out that there was a lot going on behind the swagger and the scarf. In speeches and essays, Barlow would articulate clever metaphors, such as the use of the word "frontier" to illustrate the online experience, combining terms from science fiction with the concerns of American revolutionaries to profoundly shape the expectations of growing legions of Internet users. He borrowed author William Gibson's term "cyberspace" and applied it directly to current Internet activity, setting Net experience apart as a separate place, which he would sometimes describe to the uninitiated as like "the place you are when you're on the telephone."

An essay of Barlow's, "The Economy of Ideas," was widely circulated and eventually published in *Wired* in early 1994. In it, Barlow voiced a response to growing concerns about "intellectual property." These concerns set the tone for many who read the essay, and examined today, they are impressively accurate.

If our property can be infinitely reproduced and instantaneously distributed all over the planet without cost, without our knowledge, without its even leaving our possession, how can we protect it? How are we going to get paid for the work we do with our minds? And, if we can't get paid, what will assure the continued creation and distribution of such work?

Since we don't have a solution to what is a profoundly new kind of challenge, and are apparently unable to delay the galloping digitization of everything not obstinately physical, we are sailing into the future on a sinking ship.

This vessel, the accumulated canon of copyright and patent law, was developed to convey forms and methods of expression entirely different from the vaporous cargo it is now being asked to carry. It is leaking as much from within as without.

Legal efforts to keep the old boat floating are taking three forms: a frenzy of deck chair rearrangement, stern warnings to the passengers that if she goes down, they will face harsh criminal penalties, and serene, glassy-eyed denial.

Intellectual property law cannot be patched, retrofitted, or expanded to contain the gasses of digitized expression any more than real estate law might be revised to cover the allocation of broadcasting spectrum. (Which, in fact, rather resembles what is being attempted here.) We will need to develop an entirely new set of methods as befits this entirely new set of circumstances.

Barlow also asserted that "The greatest constraint on future liberties may come not from government but from corporate legal departments laboring to protect by force what can no longer be protected by practical efficiency or general social consent."

John Barlow's sentiments ring all too true today.

2

NEW WORLD ORDER

The record industry is typically divided into the major labels and the independents. The former are bastions of wealth and prestige that have the capital to dominate the markets, from the airwaves to the chain stores, and control the networks of physical distribution. Smaller labels, while not enjoying those advantages, can be more focused and nimble, building on customer loyalty and brand recognition. Because they operate on a different scale, independents are free to take chances on artists and records that might never sell 200,000 units, the number needed for a major-label release to be considered successful. Independent labels range from fairly established players such as Epitaph, which often sells millions of copies of individual records from punk bands and free-spirited artists like Tom Waits, to some kid spending all his money to release his inspirations on the world from his basement. The "majors"—also commonly referred to as the "big five"—are Sony Music, Universal, EMI, Warner Brothers, and BMG (Bertelsmann Music Group). Together they account for more than $14 billion in yearly revenue in the U.S. market alone. The business-wide trend of corporate mergers is in full effect with these companies. The big five increasingly own many other smaller labels, some of which were once very powerful in their own right, and many of which retain a degree of autonomy. Geffen, Atlantic, and Virgin records, for instance, have been brought under the greater umbrellas of Universal, Warner, and EMI, respectively. The commonly used "indie label" moniker is a little tricky: while many independent labels are shoestring operations run out of someone's basement, often hooked into a larger distributor, others, formerly of the basement type, have been bought out and absorbed by majors, or have made some kind of distribution deal with one of them, and are thus not quite so independent.

As the record companies have become integrated within the folds of the multinational corporations that own them, in most cases business as usual has supplanted the more unsavory aura of organized crime that was earlier associated with the industry and that Fredric Dannen documented memorably in the book *Hit Men* (1991). The affectation has remained, and some, like Ice-T, insist that the business tactics haven't changed that much. "Independent promoters" who function as out-sourced bribegivers to get a song played on the radio are still used, for instance. But mostly, the old-school shakedown has been replaced with "Roman legions" of lawyers (such as those that Seagram chief Edward Bronfman Jr. threatened to unleash against the foes of copyright) and very well paid Washington lobbyists, working hard to shape laws that suit the powerful entertainment industry.

Among the majors there are strongly perceived mutual interests in many areas. The Recording Industry Association of America, or RIAA, is the trade association for the major (and many independent) labels' activities in the United States. Its main activities are the monitoring of sales to award "gold" and "platinum" record status; keeping an eye out for music bootleggers and encouraging the police to enforce laws against them; and lobbying the government to enact laws that are favorable to the industry.

The relationship of other rights bodies within the industry are relatively complex and are a fossil record that points to the past century of industry history, which was fraught with litigation and power grabs. Broadcast Music Incorporated (BMI), the American Society of

Composers, Authors and Publishers (ASCAP), and SESAC (which was once the Society of European Stage Authors and Composers, but is now simply the acronym) all license music performances, such as playing a song over the radio or in a restaurant. The royalties from these performances go to the songwriters, who are not necessarily the band playing the tune. The Harry Fox Agency, a division of the National Music Publishers' Association, oversees publishing rights to the music itself, as opposed to performances of that music. These are known as "mechanical rights." That the lengthily negotiated pacts among artists, publishers, and labels is so hard for all parties to navigate has meant that the options presented by the fast and furious world of the Net have been met with near paralysis.

From an early stage, there were people at the labels who experimented with computers. If their vision of how technology and music might meet was sometimes less inspiring than those of outsiders, it was, at least, rooted in experience. One such executive was Ted Cohen, a music biz player who became infected with the excitement of new technology.

Cohen started out at the Boston office of Warner Brothers in 1972, and he worked his way up through local promotion to artist development. By 1977 he was asked to move to Burbank to work on career development with artists such as Van Halen, Fleetwood Mac, Talking Heads, George Benson, Sex Pistols, and the Ramones. His job had all the glamorous highs and absurd lows that have become a part of the music business stereotype. Cohen would go from one week with a brand new band, driving around in a station wagon, to three months with the Who in a private plane complete with a bedroom and a shower. He dated one of the Who's flight attendants, going out for every date in a different city. Although Cohen loved the music and much of the business, after several years the personalities began to take their toll on him.

"In 1984 I went to the Beverly Center with the guys from King Crimson and saw the movie *Spinal Tap*," Cohen recounted. The next day he quit his job. "That movie was my life: on the road, dealing with dumb English bands." But by then, a seed planted earlier had begun to sprout.

In 1982, while still at Warner, Cohen had been invited to join a committee alongside vice president Stan Cornyn to talk about the intersection between technology and music. Cohen found that Cornyn, who had a solid reputation throughout many parts of the industry, "was a futurist and was into imagining what the next cool thing would be." They met to discuss ways to combine the Warner-owned (then highly successful) video game company Atari with music. They imagined discs of concerts with an assortment of bells and whistles, like guitars that changed sound with a mouse click. The committee lasted a year, until Atari got into trouble financially and was sold. But Cornyn and Cohen both still had the bug.

In 1986, Cornyn was running The Music Group, "the first interactive music label," cofounded by media and technology giant Philips, and was developing a CD-ROM and the CD-i format that would play on your television set. The latter format was abandoned once it was realized that the image quality on computer screens was much lower than required for television. Cohen joined up to work on the CD-ROM format, and in 1992, he worked on the genre-defining CD-ROM for *New World Order* by Todd Rundgren, along with unreleased prototypes for Sting and David Bowie. Cornyn experimented successfully with enhanced CDs for other bands, including The Cranberries, but after ten years The Music Group had burned through a considerable stack of cash and it was pretty clear that the format was not feasible for a mass market. In December 1996, the company shut its doors. But there was an upside: much of the research that went into fitting rock videos into music CDs proved to be valuable as Web technology developed and proliferated.

By that time, the Web was already more popular than any of the projects the labels were funding themselves. Although the music business seemed as if it would contain the perfect companies to push forth and establish outposts on the new electronic frontier, most quarters of the record industry were less than sanguine about such prospects. Moving to the Web required a much greater conceptual leap for labels than did enhanced CDs, which were sold along with standard CDs and therefore required no change in the distribution model. The online world seemed geeky, unproven, and, as The Music Group showed, you could easily lose your shirt with the stuff. But technology just kept rolling on.

In 1987, in the sleepy but prosperous Southern town of Erlangen, Germany, the Institut Integrierte Schaltungen, a part of research giant Fraunhofer, joined forces with the University of Erlangan, under Professor Dieter Seitzer, to craft an algorithm that could be used to shrink video files to a manageable size for use with multimedia. The 1980s were a long way from the modern era of cheap, fast computer processors and high-storage capacities. In order to make digital pictures play, researchers found they had to do something with the enormous media files. A "codec," short for "compression/decompression algorithm," is what was used to do the job, by smartly stripping away as much data as possible from a given file, while scientifically working to keep sound and video quality as high as possible. The Institut, and scientists such as Karlheinz Brandeburg, finally settled on the code for the audio part of their task. After the code was submitted and approved by the International Standards Organization, it became known as ISO-MPEG Audio Layer–3.

The MP3 (as the name has been commonly shortened) encoding method got its power from using perceptual, or "psychoacoustic," models that accounted for what listeners actually notice when they hear music or other sounds. Although the formula was crafted and ready to be used, it lay waiting for some kids to find it and shake things up.

* * *

While Patterson and Lord were discovering the joys of the Internet as a way of exposing The Ugly Mugs and other unsigned bands, and Cohen was developing enhanced CDs, Jim Griffin, chief technology officer at Geffen Records, was trying to build a bridge between the music industry and the Web. Griffin had moved into the world of music technology from a background in journalism. As a reporter at the

Lexington Herald-Leader in Kentucky, he developed an interest in the ways that the computer was transforming the newspaper business. This interest led him to accept a job in Washington, D.C., tracking and advising newspaper clients on the ways of new media.

Griffin was eventually hired by Geffen because he was deemed a thought-leader who could assess and explain technological options. Griffin first gained credibility by convincing the company not to release enhanced CDs. After that, when he proposed ways for Geffen to experiment with Internet promotion, company executives were willing to do so, after some initial debate. Aerosmith's unreleased "Head First" was the cut of choice. It was a giant leap for label-kind, and ironically it may have been a small step in the industry's losing some of its control: a quick search of Napster shows that "Head First" is still floating around online today. The release was a controversial move, especially when Geffen's owner, Universal, caught wind of it.

"The parent company was not pleased," said Griffin. "They knew that this sort of thing was the future, but I think their goal was to slow it down, as opposed to speed it up, and here we were speeding it up." Griffin was attempting to straddle the thin line that separated the corporate innovators from the anti-establishment.

David Weekly was on the other side of the divide that separated labels and fans. With deeply set eyes, a neat haircut, and an engaging, almost overly enunciated diction, Weekly was attending Stanford University to study computer science. It had been back at his father's office in his hometown, Boston, well before college, that Weekly first witnessed the power of the Web. In 1994, his father, a software engineer, fired up a beta version of the early Mosaic browser. Although Weekly says he was at first "unimpressed" with the infant Web, after spending a half hour downloading some "cheesy-sounding" Hungarian folk music, he became excited by the notion of online distribution. His father concluded "someone's going to make a lot of money figuring out how to compress all this stuff." Even though he was struck by the potential, Weekly didn't act on this encounter until after he graduated high school and arrived in Palo Alto.

Compared to the big-city excitement of Boston, the almost archetypal suburban sprawl of Palo Alto held few charms to engage the inquisitive Weekly. Despite being in the middle of the world's hottest spot for computer development, he found Palo Alto "not very accommodating to the college student." The town consisted mainly of "nice expensive restaurants, and nice expensive shops. There really weren't too many places an under twenty-one student could hang out." To fight the boredom, Weekly began to compose "various tunes, rhythms, jams" using software tools, a hobby he had begun in his last years at high school. After Weekly offered to share some of his compositions with a college friend, the friend suggested that he check out MP3s. Weekly had never heard of the format, but from his first download, he was bowled over by the possibilities that online music allowed.

"I'm not sure I could ever look at my computer the same way again," Weekly said. "It was now my stereo." The only thing lacking, he noticed, was somewhere reliable to find music of interest. Most of the online traders at that point relied on slow, fly-by-night FTP sites, so the work of actually tracking down music online, which usually involved finding scores of abandoned sites, made the process as maddening as it was exciting. Legitimate sites like Lord's IUMA, which offered mostly unheard-of songs by undiscovered groups, did little to alleviate Weekly's hunger for more popular music.

Having access to plenty of Stanford's bandwidth, a workable computer, and ample networking skills, Weekly decided that he would host his own site and offer choice pieces from his own music collection, along with perks such as reviews, a chat room, tech advice, and pointers to music software. Soon downloads from his small, and relatively weak, computer grew so popular that they accounted for 80 percent of the university's outgoing Internet traffic. As visitors poured in to download "Freshman" by Verve Pipe or "Jump Around" by Boston's House of Pain, suddenly Weekly was one of the rising MP3 scene's most visible figures.

While Weekly had no plans to build a company or even a career on downloadable music, his promotion of free MP3s hit a cultural nerve. Though he knew "just enough to wreak a little havoc," his site foreshadowed later developments in file sharing and served as a bridge from IUMA to Napster.

Weekly's experiment ended nearly as soon as it started. One day in 1997 Weekly got two calls from Stanford authorities. The first was from Residential Networking, wondering what on earth was responsible for hogging over 80 percent of Stanford's outgoing traffic. Then Network Security called, fresh from having spoken with a not-very-amused Geffen Records, which was upset that its songs were being served. Weekly's site was immediately shut down, the music stripped away. Still, the popularity of his site confirmed that a hunger existed for digital music, whether because it was free, convenient, or fit in with the general mania for all things Web.

On a farewell visit to his site's chat room, Weekly found it occupied solely by the vice president of technology from Geffen. Weekly noted his e-mail address, and his name, Jim Griffin. After Weekly sent an impassioned e-mail defending MP3's potential, Griffin responded that he agreed and offered Weekly his phone number.

Griffin, charming and somewhat professorial, seemed at that point to be one of the few people working in the music industry who fully understood the potential of online music, and if he was charged with the onerous task of defending copyrights, his authority was tempered by a human side. He saw the need to smooth the ugliness that could develop if the industry continued to over-protect and over-sue, and he had great insight into how Internet technologies were developing and converging. Ironically, he often had to work as the enforcer at Geffen, sending letters to sites that were posting copyrighted material, such as an enormous number of Nirvana tribute sites. Griffin asked for that task because he "didn't want the first point of contact [for fan sites] to be cops and lawyers." For Weekly, a college freshman, to hook up with the vice president of an important record company was an amazing introduction into a new world, at a pivotal time when he was taken seriously by all.

Griffin had developed relationships, both socially and technologically, with most of the developing players in online music—including Weekly, Lord, Beastie Boys' Webmaster Ian Rogers, and honchos like David Geffen. He was doing his best to forge some kind of common ground between the record industry and the technological visionaries, as well as any fans who were just trying to make sense of everything. Griffin was a frequent guest on chat sites, trying to explain Geffen's policies and promote its artists online. Given Griffin's penchant for networking, it's no surprise that one of the movers whom he and Weekly began brainstorming with was Michael Robertson, the clean-cut young entrepreneur from San Diego who had just launched MP3.com.

3

A CULTURE OF MUTATION: THE RISING INFRASTRUCTURE

M usic is a thread tightly woven within the fabric of its time. While social forces play a huge and celebrated role in its history, an equally rich story lurks beneath the developments of the electric guitar, the microphone, the distortion pedal, and the recording studio—each has played an impressive role in shaping the sounds of our culture. Music is rooted in the interaction of humans, their artifacts, and the world in which they all meet. Whether through musical scores, trumpets, electric guitars, or drum machines, technology is always present—even fundamental. By the time the recording and playback processes play their parts, and the particular medium in which a work is heard lends its context, the end result is sound that has been soaked in technology its entire length.

A shift towards synthesizers, sampling, and digital production studios means that in many cases songs nowadays are created that exist from beginning to end as purely digital code. The switch to online digital distribution fits in perfectly with these developments, just as occupations as diverse as journalist, stocktrader, and office manager have found themselves less concerned with physical objects and more concerned with playing roles within a larger datascape of networked computers. Almost all recent commercially released music has been digitally recorded, or at the very least, mastered. To go to the trouble of actually pressing a song's data onto a CD, when there are faster, more efficient ways of distributing the ones and zeroes, is increasingly anachronistic.

Even the software that plays online music, today's digitally built versions of yesterday's hi-fi, benefits from the change to networked distribution. A fundamental advantage of software over hardware when it comes to music tools like MP3 players is that even if you want to make a big update, you don't have to remold, recast, or physically reconstruct your product. Buggy software is often released in not-ready-for-primetime incarnations, while developers work to upgrade it, in hopes that users will suggest repairs or, in the case of open-source software users, actually make needed repairs themselves. If a team of programmers builds a music player that doesn't have a volume control, they don't have to scrap the program and write a new one, but simply add on as they go. Totally at odds with old-fashioned notions of materials and scarcity, once one copy is made, all others can be copied for next to nothing, and improvements spread easily, anywhere in the world.

This freedom is what drives the amazing speed and ferocious adoption rate of the software distributed on Internet. As the entertainment industry becomes increasingly high-tech, through distribution as well as production, all indications are that the pace of innovation and mutation will accelerate, at least until monopolies develop. As high-speed Net connections and powerful computers became the norm, what was true for software became true for mass media. The costs of distributing one copy of a song on the Net and 50 million of them are practically the same. The industry was slow to get its mind around this radical notion, so at odds with the fundamental economic concept of scarcity. The history of online music companies has made one thing clear: those that took advantage of the Net's most radical effects had the greatest impact. A slow and steady path that merely updated old-style marketing of scarce, expensive products meant very slow rates of consumer adoption and disappointing growth for the field. Those companies that ignored the rules—and maybe even the rule of law—succeeded in creating a mass movement.

*   *   *

If the Internet before 1995 was not exactly silent, beyond the novelty, most listening was not much fun. If you were lucky enough to have a high-speed connection at work or school, you could download songs with only a short wait. But outside that lucky circle, at a time when 14.4 kbs modems were considered hot stuff, getting music over the Net was like waiting for ketchup to flow from a new bottle: pretty frustrating if you were hungry.

By the time the Internet appeared on the covers of magazines and newspapers and had worked its way into the American consciousness, it was clear to the cognoscenti that audio on the Net would eventually be a mass phenomenon. But it seemed to most that the bandwidth commonly available to consumers could not support a mass audience for a decade. It seemed that Internet audio would only arrive after the full range of interactive TV and wired home entertainment had time to blossom.

One man wasn't willing to wait around for speedier Net connections before he shook things up. When Rob Glaser unveiled RealAudio in 1995—over two years before MP3.com was launched—something clicked. Sure, the buzzing, noisy sound of highly compressed audio was not great. But the gratification that came from listening to what you wanted without waiting an hour or two for a download, even when using a puny home modem, won streaming media a place in the hearts—and on the desktops—of many. A huge network of audio providers, including radio stations, retailers, and Web sites looking to expand their offerings, like CNET and HotWired, effectively made "Real" the Internet standard for streaming audio (and the main contender for video soon after).

Rob Glaser, the burly, sometimes confrontational former Microsoft VP, knew perfectly well how to play the standards game. He was determined to make the most of his new company, his first since resigning from Microsoft following a rumored power struggle with Nathan Myhrvold to head the company's multimedia division. For Glaser, the moment he first used the Mosaic browser, he knew he'd found something that would change everything.

"To me media is the center and the formalization of everything there is about human society," Glaser said. "Some people believe if we didn't invent first oral and then written communication, there would be no fundamental difference between us and any other species on the planet."

He believed exploiting that difference was his destiny, an obsession begun at an early age. Uniting the computer and media was his interest since at least high school. "At a core level," Glaser said, "I've always been a media junkie interested in the nexus between media communications infrastructure and interactive digital technology—the things that I'm working on now and with RealNetworks." These interests and his entrepreneurial spirit coincided to give him the inspiration to create, and doggedly work to dominate, the field. In an environment filled with college-age youths willing to lose themselves completely to their work, Glaser was able to compete because he seems to have been born with a superhuman ability to juggle an astounding number of projects. He described an "intense focus" that one sometimes sees in college kids "when they first discover that they're able to do things and have that kind of expressive impact—that you can stay up all night and write software that does something that's never been done before." Like a few other Energizer Bunny-like Microsoft alumni, Glaser has pushed himself far.

Glaser embodied some interesting contradictions, which would inevitably carry over into the company he founded. The son of a psychiatric social worker and a printer from Yonkers, New York, Glaser was tirelessly devoted to social activism from his teens, during which time he leafleted for farm workers and organized against nuclear power. At Yale, while simultaneously working for three degrees (one in computer science and two in economics), he somehow found the energy to write a column and edit the editorial page of the *Yale Daily News*, lead the Campaign Against Militarism and the Draft, and run a small videogame company called Ivy Research. By the time he graduated in 1983, Glaser was a textbook workaholic, an attribute that primed him for success at Microsoft, as well as for running the Real-Networks juggernaut.

A childhood incident seems to have set the spark that propelled him down this path. While in third grade, the young Glaser went with his New York classmates on a field trip to nearby Inwood Park, just outside the city, to visit the Native American caves where, into the '50s, one could find arrowheads.

"In addition to [the artifacts] there was a massive amount of garbage and pollution," remembered Glaser. His class was disturbed by the conditions, and his teacher encouraged them to write the parks commissioner, bundling and sending the finished complaints. The commissioner soon sent his response, a letter that quoted some of Glaser's text. The 8-year-old was very impressed by the power of interactive communication.

In high school, this fascination would continue, and while he studied early computer science, Glaser and his classmates hooked up a terrestrial wired radio station, broadcasting by stringing wires within his high school, running from a room halfway between the gym and the cafeteria. "You could argue that I'm pursuing the same interests that go back twenty years, or thirty years to third grade, only on a larger scale."

After his incredibly busy performance at school, Microsoft was the only company fast enough for Glaser. He joined the company because he was impressed with the team there, and soon he rocketed to head several key projects, picking up on some of the main technologies that would drive the Net. "I was certainly very lucky from a timing standpoint," he said, noting that he was involved with all the networking products for Microsoft in the late eighties and learned protocols such as TCP/IP (the technical underpinnings of the Internet). He was also

in charge of multimedia consumer systems, which helped him understand a fair amount about hypermedia and interactive experience
from the standpoint of the stand-alone PC.

After Glaser's departure from Microsoft, a good friend named
Mitch Kapor, inventor of Lotus 1–2–3, convinced him to join the
Electronic Frontier Foundation, which Kapor had cofounded with
John Perry Barlow, the Grateful Dead lyricist. At the EFF meetings
Glaser hooked up with Dave Farber, who would become the chief
technology officer for the Federal Trade Commission. Glaser said
about Farber: "if you use the plural, 'fathers' of the Internet, he'd cer-
tainly be in the Philadelphia Convention Hall picture."

Although Glaser also met people involved with developing interactive TV, he was not intrigued by that technology; he concluded that it
"had no method, from either a technical or from a business standpoint, of bootstrapping itself." It would not be able to take off—because it had no way of reaching the critical mass of viewer and broad-
casters interested in making it succeed. But the Net, on the other
hand, excited him with its potential. He believed it offered "an archi-
tectural solution for all the fundamental issues." Namely, the distribution network was already developed enough to sustain momentum.
"It was clear to me that through the whole phenomenon later called
viral marketing this was going to unleash incredible impact," Glaser
said. "It was one of these snowballs moving downhill with incredible
alacrity, so it seemed to me that if we could do the same thing for audio and video that Mosaic was doing for static text and images, that
we would have a profound impact."

The Web would not spring to life without baby steps, so audio—
low fidelity audio—was Glaser's way of making the first move. With
friends who had been involved in politics, he launched Progressive
Networks, a company that would deliver highly compressed sound
files in small streams so that even with slow modems, anyone could
listen in real time. The idea was to start playing the files while they
were still being downloaded, to eliminate the usual frustrating wait
before anything could be heard. The system was dubbed "Real-
Audio," using the space-less conjunction favored by Net companies.
To make it work for the slow modems of the time meant heavily

compressing the audio file, stripping away a vast amount of information and leaving only the bare bones of sound. What you ended with usually resembled a scratchy low-fi AM radio. Even with its faults, the fact that RealAudio worked was an exciting beginning, and it was actually a very apt solution for talk-based radio and news shows. While some hard-core geeks conceivably would spend a night downloading a song by their favorite groups, few would do the same for National Public Radio's "All Things Considered." But once the barrier of a huge download was eliminated, many listeners flocked to the Web to hear to their favorite shows at their convenience and search the archives of countless broadcasts.

RealAudio's main target was radio stations that wanted to make their broadcasts, usually talk, available. Glaser could see the difficulties of persuading the record labels to release their prized catalogs of songs and didn't want to pursue music downloads just yet. Comparing streaming audio files for broadcast to downloading them for physical delivery, Glaser decided for two reasons to avoid the latter. The first reason was that low-power modems made downloading too onerous for the general public. The second, more persistent issue was that the owners of copyrights were unlikely to embrace the Net, "not for reasons of rational economic self-interest, but because the music industry operated in a hidebound, one might even say cartel-like, way."

Glaser described the attitude of the major record companies as "'we have these physical pressing plants, why would we put anyone else in the distribution business?'" He could see that they didn't want to let anyone else in "even though those new people might have grown their business. So, our philosophy was: let's deliver the best possible consumer experience and focus on something that doesn't have gatekeepers that can unilaterally determine whether or not we can get something going." The reluctance of rights holders did not subside over time. Quite the contrary, he said, "now it's the battle royale."

The radio strategy worked, and soon there were stations all over the world distributing programming on the Web, from hour-long specials to around-the-clock broadcasting. Web sites like CNET and HotWired were trying to use the Net to score points over old media by supplementing their written offerings with RealAudio interviews and reporting. Despite only-adequate sound, online offerings expanded beyond talk to music radio, and RealAudio also became the default format for previewing songs on sites such as Amazon.com. It wasn't just in America, either. Envelope-pushing radio stations around the world began to broadcast their content over the Net. Expatriates from countries as far apart as Finland and Thailand were able to tune in to the music of their homelands, just as scattered American college alumni could stay tuned to their universities' stations.

Several generations later, RealAudio started to sound very good, especially over faster lines. Fidelity at slower settings was better, too. With its primacy established for streaming audio, the company next turned its focus to developing video on the Net. It changed its name to RealNetworks and filed for an IPO. On November 21, 1997, the company raised $37.5 million by selling 3 million shares.

While video was the obvious progression from audio, and dominating the field a worthy goal, the company failed to see how popular downloadable music was becoming. It wasn't until after the success of Winamp and Napster that RealNetworks would release RealJukebox, an MP3 player of its own. Though RealAudio convinced a generation of Net users that sound worked on the Web, it did not focus any efforts to build a business selling or distributing popular songs. That was where Liquid Audio stepped in.

While Santa Cruz was the lush and isolated birthplace for IUMA's portal for bands, there was another spot not far north whose rich mix of academic values, technical innovation, and do-it-yourself culture encouraged pushing all the limits of music, especially when it came to technology. If the semiconductor chip business was important enough to name the whole region "Silicon Valley," the heady musical side of Palo Alto and neighboring Redwood City and Menlo Park was busy following its own path, and one would inevitably intersect the other.

The sprawling suburbs, towns, and wooded hills southwest of the San Francisco Bay seemed to represent American innovation in the latter parts of the twentieth century. The area also defined experimentation, both technical and social, and was the birthplace of the Grateful Dead and the Jefferson Airplane, though they later moved to the urban setting of San Francisco's Haight Street. Despite plenty of upscale neighborhoods, from the sixties through the early nineties there was still room for bohemians and enclaves such as that of author Ken Kesey, whose regional "acid tests" (as well as LSD experiments conducted by Stanford) were crucial factors in launching the psychedelic movement of the sixties.

"It's a fertile area, that's for sure," said Liquid Audio CEO Gerry Kearby, pointing out that the trio of Stanford University, audio hardware manufacturer Ampex, and the Grateful Dead all combined to create an environment of audio exploration; his company brought together veterans from all three. The combination of music and the computer was simply inevitable, and there was not a more likely spot for propagation than the South Bay and its community of Deadhead engineers.

"All that stuff sort of started with the Dead. They spent a lot of money trying to figure out how to make stuff sound better, and how to push the envelope," said Kearby. "Bands like the Dead and companies like Ultrasound—the Dead's PA company—were very involved in the transition of adding computers to the process of making music."

Because Ampex "was the greatest audio company in the world in the late '70s and '80s," engineering products that are still in use today, Kearby says that the company was responsible for a convergence of audio engineers in the region. Ray Dolby, for instance, was working at Ampex when he developed his idea for noise reduction. "It's no accident that I'm here, and many top engineers at Dolby and Liquid Audio came from Stanford," said Kearby. Besides of its network of like-minded professionals with a penchant for experimentation, the environment was good for inspiration.

Kearby's contribution to the online world evolved from a rich collage of experience in the many sides of making music. He was born in Oklahoma, and his life was typical of many American rolling stones; his hometown was where he decided it would be. Though he attended college during the Vietnam War, Kearby was drafted into the Marines, losing the typical student exemption because he was too busy playing in rock bands and "forgot to go to classes." He managed to avoid a Southeast Asian tour of duty and became drummer in a Corps band. There he saw a different type of action; he was required, he says, to play drums in the middle of a Washington "riot" while an angry mob pelted him with rocks.

After his time in the service, Kearby resumed his studies at San Francisco State University without much direction—he refers to his time there as "majoring in the G.I. Bill." (Actually, he earned a B.A. in broadcast management and audio engineering.) Back in San Francisco he helped some friends manage a recording studio and found that he enjoyed the work. Kearby became a sound engineer for bands like Jefferson Starship and the Grateful Dead until "after a couple of years it occurred to us that we were doing all the work, and the musicians were getting all the money." During this period he was also actively teaching music to marching bands, a vocation he practiced for ten years.

In the mid-'80s, as easy-to-use personal computers like the Apple Macintosh were gaining popularity, Kearby and some friends from the Center for Computer Research in Music and Acoustics at Stanford realized that there would be a market for computer-controlled recording studios. They formed a company called Integrated Media Systems, which was quickly tapped by George Lucas to build his first professional digital recording studio. Kearby describes the development as almost happening by itself: "one day we woke up and found ourselves a high technology company." By 1989, the company sold his digital audio workstation to the Swiss firm Studer Editech, and Kearby stayed on as VP of sales and marketing. After several years, he grew restless. In 1995, Kearby quit his job, and took the summer off to "walk the dog and watch the O. J. trials."

By then the hype over the Internet had grown into a roar and was quickly becoming an American obsession. Whether walking the dog or watching TV, few Bay Area residents escaped the powerful buzz. Kearby was no exception, and with plenty of sound technology experience under his belt, he realized that he knew how to make "the kind of authoring tools that everyone on the Internet needed." He had heard the streaming offered by Glaser's RealAudio and thought it was "OK," but realized that musicians and labels would soon want to sell songs and records on the Net and that this business—worth potentially billions of dollars—would require special tools. He believed that he could build those tools.

Kearby quit walking his dog so much and recruited a friend, the software engineer Phil Wiser, also from Integrated Media Systems, and venture capitalist Robert Flynn. They began developing the Liquid software and went in search of the right venture company for financing. They believed Hummer Winblad to be that company—because of its reputation as a smart investor that took a hands-off approach after assembling the management team—but roping the company in would prove difficult. Kearby and Wiser originally thought that their system would need a hardware component, in addition to their software tools; something with added processing power to decrypt sound while retaining high quality. Hummer Winblad was a software-only firm and declined to even hear their pitch.

When a self-imposed deadline for launching his company or finding another job was just a month away, Kearby read an ad in the paper announcing that venture capitalist Ann Winblad would soon make an appearance at San Jose's nonprofit Center for Software Development (now known as the Software Development Forum). This was a fundraiser—casually called "The Gong Show"—at which developers paid a nominal fee to talk to a VC for ten minutes, with all proceeds benefiting the center. Kearby called the center the day before the event and was told that the event had been sold out for months. He asked if anyone might have canceled. Nope. Realizing that this was probably a needy group of developers, Kearby had the bright idea to inquire if anyone's check had bounced. Sure enough, one had, and he was able to assume that place.

His presentation went well, and on second meeting Winblad told him that although she liked his ideas, he was clearly "an audio guy" who "didn't think like us Silicon Valley people." He needed some help polishing his pitch. She suggested that he hook up with Steve Holtzman. A latter-day Renaissance man and a connected Silicon Valley player, Holtzman juggled careers as an avant-garde composer and digital theorist. An unimposing figure with sharp, darting eyes, Holtzman had held successive positions as VP of marketing at Wise and Radius, and he'd earned a lot through their successful IPOs.

As one who'd often contemplated music's place on the Net, Holtzman was immediately enticed. He called Kearby that day and met him the next. After lending a quick hand to polish Kearby's plan, Holtzman ended up writing a check for $100,000 on the spot. Kearby phoned Winblad to relay the good news. "I said 'Hey, Ann, your due diligence guy just wrote me a check. Let's do this deal,'" Kearby remembered. Though she was obviously keen on the deal, Winblad put Kearby through an "Excalibur test" by seeing if he could strike an exclusive deal with Dolby labs. Through years of work, Kearby was very familiar with the key figures at Dolby and had good relationships there. But the company was known to refuse any exclusive deals, and so it came as a surprise that Kearby instantly snagged the exclusive Internet rights to use Dolby's encoding technology. Hummer Winblad put together a $2 million deal that included $600,000 from Intel, and Liquid was launched in May 1996.

By November, the company assembled a product that did not require any additional hardware and set out to show it to the world. Sammy Hagar, fresh out of Van Halen, a friend of Kearby's, offered to put up a single from his first post–Van Halen album, *Salvation on Sand Hill*. Both Hagar and Liquid were happy with the consumer response. "The reaction was pretty immediate at the pro-media level," Kearby said, claiming 100,000 downloads for the song. There was an added benefit of generating that same number of addresses for a Hagar e-mailing list. This list concept was key in strengthening artists' abilities to market themselves and loosen the grip of the industry. "We saw the Internet as a way for musicians to be able to sell their music without having to get record contracts," said Kearby.

The Liquid system was threefold. There was the encoding software, called the Liquifier, which used the AAC compression, a stronger, better-sounding format than MP3. To send Liquid files over the Net, the Liquid Music Server was needed. In addition to standard file-server functions, the Server encrypted every music file and slapped a watermark in it for good measure. Only those listeners with a Liquid Music Player positively identified as the owner of a certain song were allowed to play it. If anyone else tried, they were redirected to a commerce site where they might purchase a copy for themselves.

Once a song was downloaded, listeners were allowed to burn one copy to a CD, provided they had such a burner. Overall, what customers got was a process that left them with pretty much what they would get if they bought their music at a record store, minus a little sound quality and the CD booklet. Liquid Audio made retailers nervous, but was still familiar to the industry compared to much of the Net, inasmuch as it spoke a language that retailers were familiar with and changed the business in terms they understood. When Liquid launched, MP3 was still essentially underground.

Despite tools such as e-mail registration that would help artists to control their own marketing, Liquid was very careful not to rock the boat within the establishment and worked hard to stay on friendly terms with everyone.

"When I started the company I had a mantra that was: 'empower those in power,'" said Kearby. "It just seemed like such a complex food chain that almost anybody could veto you. When we started, my partners Rob and Phil and I diagrammed the music food chain and made sure that the Internet provided a positive value proposition for everyone from the recording studio owner, through the distributor, through the collection agency through the retailer and then ultimately the consumer. We were often accused of doing too much, but when you're inventing an industry . . . . It wasn't like Henry Ford had any choice but to put four wheels on a car. You've got to do the whole thing."

Liquid Audio's insistence on copy protection and other industry-friendly gestures still did not appease all quarters. The industry remained wary. Kearby presented a demo—a song produced by the legendary hit man Phil Ramone—at the offices of online music retailer N2K (later acquired by CDNow). Kearby took the group through all the steps: paying for the song, downloading and then burning it to disc, just as Liquid Audio hoped consumers would. Playing the CD back and comparing it to the original on "a very high-quality set of speakers" impressed everyone. Ramone himself, Kearby related, turned to him and said, "This is gonna piss a lot of people off!"

The people that Liquid was most likely to disturb were the ones who had the most to lose from an Internet sales model: the brick-and-mortar retailers who weren't set up to sell on the Web. In September 1997, their fears were stoked. Capitol records planned to release "Electric Barbarella," a single from a new album by the '80s new wave glamour boys Duran Duran. The company wanted not only to release the single in the Liquid format, but also, contrary to advice by Liquid, release it online—before it made it to retail. The retailers were immediately displeased. Phil Ramone was right: The Net has the capability of offending, or disintermediating, everybody. Capitol backed down after retailers threatened to boycott the CD, and the song was released on the Net and in stores simultaneously. Retailers needn't have worried so much: few consumers were receptive to buying music through such an untested system, and nothing very sexy was there to lure them to experiment.

Although Glaser's RealNetworks and Kearby's Liquid Audio achieved their own brand and degree of success, neither company was prepared for the tidal wave that MP3 rode in on. And while being tied so heavily to their own proprietary system may prove to be a long-term blessing, as the wealth of MP3-based innovation began to spring up around the Web, it was hard to see the format as anything but a curse, especially for Liquid, which was such a direct competitor. Until 1999, only the Liquid Player could play its specialized format. While the Player had loads of great features, including the ability to display cover art and integrate commerce, it was next to impossible to get music fans to download and install it when they had such a wide choice of other, more enticing options. Namely, free music.

*   *   *

If the successive waves of online music pioneers included many who were pushing the technological, social, and legal limits for a mixture of aesthetic hopes and utopian dreams, what pushed MP3.com founder Michael Robertson was something different. He hadn't cared very much about music since ending a brief stint playing clarinet in his high school band, and the first time he even noticed the term MP3s was when he saw how popular it was as a search word on a Web site he was running. But Robertson was a natural-born capitalist.

"Well, you know, I grew up really poor," Robertson said once in an unguarded moment. "I think that has a way of motivating people, and

I do have the entrepreneurial bug. Hopefully, after three companies, maybe I got it right with MP3.com."

Blond, boyish-looking, and with the constantly upbeat manner of a salesman or a preacher, Robertson grew up in San Diego, California, in a very religious family with modest means. Not interested in more of the same for himself and his kids, Robertson meticulously transformed himself into a notoriously hard-driven entrepreneur. After receiving his B.A. in cognitive science from University of California San Diego, he jumped into the world of high tech by starting two successive software companies, MR Mac and Media Minds. The first was a networking and security consultancy, for which his enthusiasm faded when he realized how hard it was to scale to something really big. Software didn't have that limitation—although one body could only do so much consulting, one program could travel anywhere. Media Minds made imaging software, tools for managing digital photos; it wasn't very successful, Robertson contended, because it was ahead of its time. To have that much experience under his belt while not yet thirty was priceless.

His third enterprise, The Z Company, was an umbrella for several Web sites, run out of his garage, that enabled different types of Net searches. It was while looking at the logs of Filez.com that Robertson noticed that the term "MP3" was incredibly popular. A little research convinced him that this was something that he should pursue. One idea and a thousand bucks later he had bought the MP3.com domain. In November 1997, Robertson launched the MP3.com Web site.

Stanford student David Weekly's new site, the MP3 Audio Consortium, or M3C, meanwhile, was getting many thousands of visitors a day, and the movement was growing among college students and hardcore Net enthusiasts, attracted to the growing ease and fun of swapping songs over the Internet. MP3.com and the MP3 Audio Consortium shared a common mission. But Robertson wanted music, and he wanted it legally. There were a lot of music Web sites, but not many had full songs, at least not with the permission of musicians.

"None of us were musicians, we didn't know any musicians, and we didn't have any money to buy record label rights digitally. We started focusing attention on getting a list of bands," Robertson said. He scoured the Net for any bands that had music online and found the selection to be widely dispersed, like "one jazz band in Sweden, one reggae band in Canada." Robertson linked to them, but because the music was hosted on each band's own site, download problems were common. It dawned on Robertson that he could make the whole system more reliable if he hosted the music himself, and so he sent out personal invitations to any band he could find, calling them to say, "Would you let us make a Web site for you? It will be faster than your current Web site, and it won't cost you anything. After a while, we didn't even have to tell anybody."

As far as the exclusive rights that a record label or other online sites would later demand, Robertson said it never dawned on him. "We said all this craziness about good contracts, bad contracts, contracts that artists couldn't get out of for ten years—let's just make it so that an artist can leave whenever they want to and take all their music with them." It's doubtful that many artists would have given up their exclusive rights for free, anyway, so nonexclusivity let MP3.com grow without concern.

MP3.com—largely due to its domain name—soon became *the* gathering post for people interested in online music. Descriptions of what the format did made it easy for newbies to jump right in. The latest software tools were reviewed, and linked to; and a database of songs from any bands who wanted to offer their music was posted to show that MP3 was not just for musical pirates. In February 1998, Robertson tossed around an idea with his new friends online, including David Weekly and a manager named John Parres, about hosting a small gathering to promote and discuss MP3.

Weekly had been planning to host a conference of his own, set for the fall of 1997, and had even been promised a sponsorship by the RIAA. "They claimed that their vision was 'education first, then litigation,' so I took them to task on it," Weekly said. His main desire was that the event would remain cheap and open to the creative poor students and slackers who were driving the movement. But the RIAA eventually backed out, and Weekly canceled his event, passing the torch to Robertson. The MP3 summit was officially announced on the MP3.com site.

To help spread the word about the event and the site, Robertson needed a publicist. With the help of John Parres, Robertson settled on a young Hollywood PR gun, Hal Bringman. Bringman threw his all into the MP3.com project, his first independent job after leaving his job at an agency, and became instrumental in spreading the word. It helped that he understood the company's objectives. "I had done enough work with bands to know that things needed to improve for them," he said. "When you've gotten enough calls from a bass player in Boise, freaking out because his band isn't being given any support from the label, it's easy to see how the industry should change."

Robertson's event was planned to be just "some kind of slumber party where you order a pizza" and talk with a few other enthusiasts. He didn't expect the phenomenal response the announcement received. In a few weeks time, the number of attendees had jumped from twenty to five hundred. Record industry and high-tech big shots, and even a member of Congress, were pledging to attend. Hasty plans were made to host the event at the University of California San Diego, which lent an inquisitive, collegiate, and friendly air to the meeting.

The conference was a heady moment for those who had latched on to the promising new way of getting music over the Net, and a strong buzz could be felt. For years, Webheads had speculated about being able to get music at the touch of a button over the Internet, and now the moment they'd been waiting for seemed at hand. David Weekly described feeling "like a Scotsman in *Braveheart*."

Robertson leaped onto the college auditorium stage; he was riding high on the excitement and seemed most thrilled by the variety of people attracted to the summit. He praised MP3 as a "collective effort, from kids in high school to men in business."

"Back in those days, guys at these companies that would later be considered rivals were talking to each other on the phone every day," remembered Bringman. "Companies like MP3.com, Emusic (then Goodnoise), and Musicmatch. There was a lot of mutual support."

Perhaps it was just the shock of instantly becoming players in a business that had seemed so far out of reach, but the hacker developers of the MP3 revolution displayed a remarkable amount of respect and empathy for the record industry. Rather than gloating over newfound power with threatening bravado, most of the speakers that day seemed to bend over backwards to suggest ways for record labels to make money.

Winamp announced that it was adding links from its player to CD marketers, hoping to build "as many legitimate routes to music distribution as we can, to supplement the already heavily saturated pirate market." Hassan Miah, CEO of Xing, makers of software to encode standard music into MP3 files, pointed out that the labels stood to make a lot of money by reselling their back catalog on MP3, as they had with CDs.

Although the summit was about MP3, there were representatives of other formats, chiefly Liquid Audio, on hand to maintain a presence and keep an eye on things. They must have sensed the danger of being eclipsed by MP3's popularity. Founder Gerry Kearby had been pushing Liquid's own proprietary compression scheme for a few years, schmoozing the record industry while gathering financing and hoping to be in the right position when the market for online music arrived in earnest. Kearby and company continued to heavily promote its security features that kept consumers from freely distributing duplicates. MP3, in contrast, was an open standard, which encouraged developers to implement whatever brainstorms they had for new players or components, and its lack of security elements attracted legions of devoted users. Thanks to MP3.com and a few other emerging players, the future that Liquid Audio had been counting on was suddenly in danger of disappearing. Even so, Liquid's spokesman, Richard Fleischman, kept a brave face and called the times "exciting," because "everyone feels that the way music is distributed is about to change."

That something big was occurring wasn't lost on the media. Before the summit, it was very difficult to get the ear of any journalists, said Bringman. "It was just News.com and Wired News." Afterwards, the media buzz quickly rose. The record labels, though, did not seem to reciprocate either the friendliness or the optimism that the MP3 summit inspired.

In three weeks' time, Robertson would find himself the outsider at a music industry event that couldn't have been timed better to serve as a foil to the unbridled optimism of the fall summit. At "Downloadable

Music: Revolution or Revitalization?" held by the Los Angeles chapter of the Recording Academy, a panel was stacked with insiders ready to fight for every ounce of control they had, along with a few groveling multimedia companies there to show they understood who was boss.

From the outset it was clear that this was not your typical Internet panel: Instead of a Spartan college campus, this discussion was at the posh Nikko hotel in Hollywood. Perfume wafted heavily through the room and there wasn't a software T-shirt in sight. A huge golden gramophone was perched at the side of the stage, lest anyone forget that the Recording Academy was the group that awards the Grammies. The panel, drawn from a wide variety of music publishers, distributors, and retailers, had one thing in common: a heavily vested interest in the status quo. The two new media companies represented were Liquid Audio, which had gone to great pains to present itself as the answer to any fears the industry might be having about the Internet, and IUMA, which, being concerned almost exclusively with helping unsigned artists market themselves, was little threat to anyone.

Michael Green, president and CEO of the academy, started the evening by noting that with downloadable music, "the stakes are incredibly high." He should have known: as head of the "nonprofit" academy, he was making a very comfortable living. In fact, the discrepancy between his position and his income he was a frequent subject for the *Los Angeles Times*, which reported that he "drives a Mercedes-Benz, enjoys a membership at the Bel-Air Country Club and makes $1.3 million a year—all at the expense of the academy and its charitable arms," and was, according to its sources, the target of a fruitless federal tax investigation.

The shared message that the panelists imparted that night was succinctly articulated by Mike Farrace, the vice president of Tower Records, who warned against Internet users' naïve presumption, declaring that the freedom the Internet offered shouldn't be taken as an exemption from financial responsibilities. "It's time that we show people that if you want the free goodies, you're going to have to pay!" he said. The spirit was there, even if the precise logic wasn't.

Albhy Galuten, vice president of interactive programming at Universal Music Group, also reflected a shared astonishment and frustration over young people's disregard for intellectual property. Galuten, a producer with credits that include *Saturday Night Fever* and a host of others, stressed, and other panelists repeated, an almost desperate need to educate consumers about intellectual property.

While the panel itself seemed chosen less to foster debate than to deliver a group message, when the floor opened for questions, the panelists steeled themselves against an onslaught. What the audience lacked in tech savvy it made up for with direct industry experience—Hollywood was home base for artists as well as industry bosses.

Among the first to speak was music attorney Ken Hertz, whose laid-back beachcomber appearance belied his power as dealmaker for Hollywood stars like Will Smith, Alanis Morissette, and Courtney Love. How, he asked the panel, did these company men get off saying that they were so interested in preserving artists' profits? Of course, he pointed out, artists would try alternate routes—they've got almost nothing to lose from the standard record deal. Everyone with a record contract knows that artists make almost no money from selling records. Industry opposition to the Internet, he suggested, was motivated by greed, and cloaking it as concern for artists' rights wouldn't fly when the artists started turning away.

When Michael Robertson rose to the microphone it seemed like less than half of the panelists knew who he was, and those who did viewed him as little more than riffraff. Robertson pointed out that the software industry had learned to deal with piracy, and even use it as a way of establishing dominant market share; the music industry, he suggested, should learn to do the same. When told by the moderator to ask a question of the panel and not make speeches, Robertson summed up his position by saying that the music industry should stop seeing the Internet community as a threat. "We're here to embrace you," he said, arms outreached, smiling beatifically.

"That may be so," responded the RIAA representative, a stand-in for president Hillary Rosen, who'd canceled her appearance. The RIAA man was much older than everyone else on the panel and had spoken that night with a bitter aloofness that suggested he had much better things to be doing. "But we're not interested in embracing just anyone," he said with a look of distaste. The evening ended on that sour note.

Robertson's presence at the academy panel was for a larger purpose than simply networking. He was building a one-man brand. Bringman described a plan they developed to make Robertson synonymous with online music. "We worked hard to make sure that he was at every event, and would appear in every important story. Even if he wasn't speaking he was there asking questions." The public abuse and private scorn was not pleasant, but it seemed not to faze Robertson at all. With no background in the music business, he gave little thought to making friends. "I remember having conversations after he'd come from being slammed, and he'd just say, 'that was brutal,' but I think the opposition just fed his fire and made him that much more determined," Bringman observed.

Robertson's public persona certainly echoed that assessment, and in interviews he would inevitably joke about the unpleasantness. "Some of my contacts up in L.A. say, 'Michael, you know they think you're Satan, right?'" he related to a San Diego paper. "I say 'I'm blond—I can't be Satan.'" He would take pains to preserve that blond angelic look, and could sometimes be seen in quiet moments before conferences spritzing his hair in the shadow of his limousine.

The strategy of ubiquity worked beautifully. A domain named after an exciting new technology, combined with a constant presence in the press, made the distinct impression on many casual, and some more active, observers that Michael Robertson was the man behind the MP3 phenomenon. "People really thought that because he owned the domain MP3.com, that he was responsible for the software, that he was Fraunhofer," Bringman said. "It was either the world's greatest scam, or just a wonderful misunderstanding."

Of course, it was not unlike Robertson to puff up more than his hair if it helped his business. As MP3.com entered a silent period in anticipation of an initial public offering, few outside of the music labels questioned Robertson's role as *de facto* spokesman for the movement. But Bringman, at least in retrospect, said he was not entirely impressed with the reality behind the swagger. "He kept telling me that we'd beat the labels because we had the technology. But when it came to technology all they had, really, were a couple of CGI scripts." That is, only the underpinnings of a Web site, not a rare commodity.

As some of the entrepreneurial camaraderie faded, a mutual bitterness had developed, too, between Liquid and MP3.com. "When MP3.com came along, we sort of saw them as sort of bullshit," Kearby recalled, labeling the company's argument that unprotected MP3 would make a musician's career better "just nonsense." He said that Robertson had "vilified" Liquid and "jumped all over me because I wanted to protect the property of the property owner."

"I spent all this time building technology so that musicians could make a living, and here's Michael Robertson saying 'just give it away and let me make the advertising revenue and somehow the glory will pass on to you.'" Kearby said Liquid tried to be friendly with MP3.com "because we liked the idea that they had a lot of musicians," but over time the animosity surfaced, and he decided to "go after artists with a more professional approach."

Designing its product in a way that seemed geared to cover every possible objection raised by the big labels, and taking on the unenviable task of trying to lead the fearful by the hand into the digital realm, earned Liquid Audio a reputation as an industry brownnoser, just as Robertson was doing his best Mr. Smith Goes to Hollywood. In a world that put a high value on outsiders, Liquid's response was less than convincing: "Our company is being portrayed as lackeys to the record industry's Evil Empire," Kearby told an *Upside* reporter. "But that's not at all what we're about. We're a technology company that's laying down the rail lines for record companies and artists to get to the Internet."

Whether it was laying rail or bending over backwards to placate all parties, it was a predicament that Rob Glaser had wanted RealNetworks to avoid. "We looked at the early secure things, the Liquid Audios and their ilk, and we came to feel that the problem was that those entities, because they would be 100 percent beholden to the rights holders, might not ever get off the ground," Glaser said. "They were certainly going to burn a substantial and fundamentally unpredictable amount of money trying to get off the ground."

And while Liquid was busy building a railway, most folks online preferred to drive their own car, steering it wherever they preferred. Because the Liquid Player wouldn't handle MP3s, just as online music was suddenly developing a real audience through the MP3 format, most listeners found that Liquid wasn't worth the trouble of installation. The company reluctantly added MP3 compatibility to its player in 1999. Kearby still firmly believed that time was on his side. "We're proponents of 'slow and steady wins the race,'" he said. MP3 sites and file trading software such as Napster were "winning the war giving away stuff, but we don't really want to win that war. We sell our stuff . . . that's a real business."

*   *   *

In 1996, while Hummer Winblad was busy putting a financing deal together for Liquid Audio, 19-year-old Justin Frankel needed a job—his mother and father said so. But his hometown, the picturesque, outdoorsy new age Mecca of Sedona, Arizona, had little to offer by way of employment, and Frankel spent most of his time chatting online and working on software projects. His latest was an MP3 player that was attracting a large audience because of its ease of use and clever features that made users feel more like they were using a stereo than computer program. Frankel was giving it away for free, helping to feed the scene growing around the suddenly popular format.

Meanwhile, Rob Lord, who had left his founding job at IUMA to work at online music company N2K, was eyeballing Frankel's work.

N2K was good for Lord's book of contacts; in a town of important people it had helped him have a reputation as an important player. But if he had a complaint, it was that the company was ignoring the realities developing on the Internet; it pursued deals that paled in comparison to what he could foresee. Those feelings came to a head when he was asked to help organize a deal with Liquid Audio.

"For everything they were doing, I didn't believe it was going to work at Liquid, it was too top-down," Lord recounted. Liquid simply didn't have a critical mass of users. Instead, Lord was watching something else grow, an Internet community of MP3 users that were persuaded by the friendly charms of Frankel's player. He told his colleagues, "This teenager named Justin who's invented the first MP3 player to use a graphic user interface, a playlist, and EQ—he's done all these amazing firsts. We should be in this space, figuring out how to leverage this." It fell on deaf ears, he found. "They couldn't understand what I was talking about."

Fed up with naysayers, in early 1997, Lord got in touch with Frankel himself and proposed collaboration. Frankel was agreeable but wanted to see just the value Lord might be able to offer. Advertising was the first thing on Lord's list. It was an easy sell because of the huge traffic coming to Frankel's site in search of software, and Lord quickly inked a $300,000 deal with the just-launched music merchandising site Artist Direct. Frankel was impressed, but the reality of the situation made him a little nervous.

"Suddenly Justin doesn't know what to do. He says, 'I need to talk to someone about what we're going to do with this business; I need to talk to my dad.' So he talks to his dad, and then soon comes back with 'My dad is talking to my mom.'" Lord got to work crafting a pitch to convince the parental units, with help from some local connections he'd made in Sedona. "We put together a white paper that said: 'If Justin continues to do what he's doing he could be a millionaire; if he turns it into a company it could turn into something much bigger.'"

Mom, Dad, and Justin were convinced, and they hired Lord as soon as the first advertising check came in. Lord packed up and moved to Sedona, which was "like living in the Grand Canyon." They quickly hired a Frankel pal and whiz developer, Tom Pepper, and also Ian Rogers, chief of technology for the Beastie Boys, who shared vision, technical skills, and a great set of contacts. While Rogers proved to be a great evangelist on behalf of the company, the scene really did have a life of its own. Rogers credits Lord with building something sustainable out of the company.

Although now known perhaps infamously as the company that unleashed the Napster-in-waiting—Gnutella—on the world, Frankel's Nullsoft started as a maker of an MP3 software player called Winamp. In two years, the pet project of an almost aimless teen would become one of the crown jewels in the biggest media merger of all time.

"One of the reasons I moved from N2K to Nullsoft is because I realized that you could build a bridge from Winamp's pirating scene, if we could create a minibrowser that would let you buy the CD you're listening to," Lord said. Plans also included plug-ins that would allow Winamp to play secure formats. "If you could listen to those as easily as you could your MP3s then maybe we could create a legitimate commercial digital distribution market." Those were some of the main things that Lord did when he joined Nullsoft, working with an eye towards pushing Justin to bridge the MP3 scene with real Internet music market opportunities. "The idea was to be agnostic."

Months after Michael Robertson's Hollywood brush-off, in October 1998, another company hoping to make a splash with consumers was clashing with the old guard. Until that point, the only portable, Walkman-like devices that would play MP3s were manufactured in either Korea or Germany, and sales were well outside the standard consumer electronics route.

Diamond Multimedia had the idea that the time was right for a mass-market version of these players and was gearing up to market its entry, the Rio. The company hoped to hit the stores with its player in time for Christmas that year, but the RIAA had other plans and hit Diamond with a lawsuit. The industry association went after Diamond for failure to comply with the Audio Home Recording Act of 1992, which forces manufacturers of digital recorders to pay a 2 percent royalty to make up for the ease-of-piracy that digital recording allows. Manufacturers must also implement serial copy protection within their units, which would prevent many generations of copies from being produced without a decrease in quality—the record industry's great fear with digital media.

The protection would have been impossible to add to the portable Rio player and still ship in time for Christmas—Diamond's plan. But the RIAA seemed much less concerned with getting its cut of the action than with shutting down the operation in general, or at least delaying its release until the record industry could figure out *en masse* what it was going to do with online music. RIAA chairman Hillary

Rosen, with others from the association, said that they thought the introduction of MP3 players in the consumer electronics market would kill the chances for a "legitimate" market to develop.

The legal actions heightened the sense that the RIAA was beginning to act like a bully and strengthened bonds in the MP3 community. A coterie of supporters were on hand to file support for Diamond, including Goodnoise (later Emusic) chief Robert Kohn, who declared that Rio "serves an important purpose for my company, giving consumers the opportunity to hear music in a mobile environment." He called the RIAA's lawsuit a "smear campaign" and a "smokescreen." Further, his statement painted a picture that RIAA greed was the main motivation behind the lawsuit.

"RIAA does not represent artists or composers," Kohn said. "It does not stand for the creative aspects of the recording industry. It stands primarily for the large commercial interests. The advent of the Internet has threatened the RIAA's most powerful members for reasons it leaves unspoken."

Hal Bringman was also in the courtroom, ready to direct any interested media parties to Michael Robertson, who was happy to echo Kohn's complaints against the recording industry, calling its control of audience a stranglehold. "We're talking about fundamentally changing how [consumers] buy their music, how much music they buy, and how they listen to their music. Amazon isn't changing how you read books; we are changing how you listen to music, where you listen to it, what music you listen to, and how artists get paid. That kind of radical change, I would suggest, makes the music industry the most impacted by the Internet of any industry in the world."

While a preliminary injunction was granted in U.S. District Court in Los Angeles, halting distribution of the Diamond's Rio player, Judge Aubrey Collins reversed her decision a few days later on October 27. Diamond's case was aided by the submitted testimony of James M. Burger, a Washington lawyer who had been part of Apple's legal team from 1987 to 1996. An expert in intellectual-property policy, he had helped to craft the Audio Home Recording Act.

Burger's testimony, a copy of which appeared on the Web site MP3.com, asserted that the RIAA "gave an inaccurate account of the legislative history of the AHRA." Only if the Rio could accept input from a consumer-electronics device—like a stereo—would it be covered by the act, he said. Since the Rio was designed to record from a computer, the statute would exempt the player.

The RIAA reps were crestfallen and tried hard afterwards to shake off their image as lawsuit-happy philistines. The makeover campaign was cut short, however, by the pressing need to go after each successive Internet threat. It was hard to appear pro-technology when every innovation seemed to threaten their hold over distribution and later threatened even copyright, the foundation of all the association's legal work.

The growing ranks of Web sites distributing legitimate MP3s were as happy as Diamond itself with the outcome of the lawsuit. They were betting heavily that sales of the Rio players would lead to increased consumer activity and a domestication of the MP3 format— eventually leading enthusiasts to actually pay for their online tunes. But that would have to wait. Christmas '98 did not sell as many players as expected, and sales did not improve through 1999. Consumers, it seemed, were not ready to fully commit themselves to the evolving parameters of online music, unless it was easy and free.

Pushing the parameters was, unfortunately, not on the agenda of the Secure Digital Music Initiative either. Started by the RIAA, the SDMI was intended to be the industry's technologically savvy rebuttal to what it perceived as pervasive lawlessness online. Heading the initiative was an Italian scientist, Leonardo Chiariglione, who had previously worked on the Motion Picture Experts Group (MPEG) and with it had helped give birth to MP3. SDMI was his attempt to tame the beast. The clock was ticking, but after many meetings it seemed that all that the representatives of the biggest companies in the world could do was schmooze and swagger, each refusing to compromise. Danger was lurking, but there was currently little profit disruption. Having overcome the shakeups and downturns of the '80s, and a notable mid-'90s slump, a combination of mergers and cost-cutting had put the industry in better financial shape than ever before. The status of most artists, though, was as shaky as ever.

4

BIG BREAKS AND WINDFALLS

Asking what the Net might mean to artists in the long run is likely to provoke varied responses—it's clear that it is a vital tool, but its uses range from the banal to the sublime, with a lot in between. The bottom line is that musicians need listeners, and the Web is shaping up to be the best thing yet at connecting, organizing, and sometimes marketing to like-minded people. Most of the world's musicians toil for years in obscurity, and most songwriters pen works that never leave their bedrooms. A smile and a tapping leg from fans may be enough to keep a musician going for some time, and a larger pool from which to find a responsive audience is probably the first thing that attracts musicians to the Net.

As a group, the major labels treated technology such as CDs and Minidiscs as gifts that were theirs to dole out, in measured doses, with each shot giving just enough of a lift to fuel a consumer spending spree. A nice, even progression was the key to longevity, especially at large corporations that were kept afloat in bad times through the selling and repackaging of back catalogues. The CD format, developed jointly (and semi-contentiously) by Philips and Sony and released in 1981 had, together with some notable recording successes, lifted the industry out of a recession that had plagued it since the late '70s. Consumers hoping to modernize their collections replaced their LPs with CDs at considerable expense. A higher sales price for the compact disc—which was soon cheaper to produce than vinyl—greatly increased revenue, and record stores were persuaded to drop their stock of LPs. Large chains complied almost immediately, forcing consumers to shell out for the more expensive goods. Encouraged by the much-touted archival qualities of compact discs, those consumers with the cash to do it not only traded in their old copy of their favorite records, they also frequently bought into the wave of boxed, multi-CD retrospectives. At the time, some label insiders argued in support of protective tools, such as watermarks, that would help prevent bootlegging of the CDs, but the arguments were dismissed as not worth the effort—a decision that would return to haunt all parties.

In 1981, just as the industry was busy congratulating itself for its slam dunk with CDs, a group of mavericks at Warner American Express Satellite Entertainment Company (WASEC), led by twenty-nine-year-old Bob Pittman, was able to maneuver through a moment of industry weakness to claim first-mover advantage in a valuable new industry. MTV, it happens, was launched completely outside of the industry's control. Almost overnight, labels and their artists were forced to shell out big bucks to produce lavish videos, which generated substantial advertising revenue for MTV. The revenue model was based on radio; Pittman argued that videos were free advertising for the labels' acts—something the labels desperately needed at the time. That the outsiders of WASEC could execute such a stunning coup left a lingering sore spot with record executives.

The loss of control and the missed opportunity was mourned by record companies for many years. Still, putting aside the lens of resentment, one can easily make a case that the industry was strengthened and revitalized by MTV. Highly choreographed videos such as Michael Jackson's *Thriller* attracted so many fans that they helped sell

20 million records in the United States alone, single-handedly pulling CBS records out of a downward spiral. Of course, the new preoccupation with expensive eye candy *did* up the ante for new artists in search of the big time—to the tune of at least $200,000 per video. If their experience in the '80s left the industry off balance, what happened next, in the '90s, knocked it off its feet.

The world before the Web was simply different, an era when consumers might have gone along with the slow drip of new technologies the industry had in mind for them. But after a decade of tech industry hype, beginning with Apple's famous Orwellian 1984 Super Bowl ad, in which the personal computer was presented as a force against Big Brother, consumers took to heart the urgings towards self-liberation, sometimes against originators' wishes. If a technology was moving too slowly, or its restrictions seemed overbearing, the tools to fix the problem were in easy reach: many sat on everyone's desktop. Whether building an MP3 player that did just what was wanted, or making another format that did more than MP3 offered, tinkering with the system to make it fit specific needs and desires was the order of the day. That's a difficult perspective for those previously used to setting the terms of every deal. For those who were used to accepting any offer they could get—the artists—access to tools meant that acceptance or rejection by the star makers was stripped of some of its career-crushing gravity.

Rolling Stones guitarist Keith Richards has told of an incident in the Stones' early days, when the band went to record in the studio of Chess records, the American R&B label on which many of the band's black heroes had released records. Upon arrival, the band was flabbergasted to meet one of its favorites, blues great Muddy Waters. But equally perplexing, the group found that instead of recording, advising, or producing, Waters, due to his slow record sales, was given the job of painting the studio roof. As Richards told *Guitar Player* magazine, the message couldn't be clearer: "Welcome to the music business!" At least Waters had some form of income. Many musicians of his era had been left high and dry by unscrupulous publishers and agents; many died penniless while their music continued to generate profits for the owners who had obtained its copyright.

The Internet in the '90s became a playground and a laboratory for musicians. The major players were usually veterans like David Bowie, the Beastie Boys, or Chuck D, who had plenty of experience working within the system and little to lose if their Web efforts failed. They were able to use firsthand knowledge about what was working and what was deficient in the system, especially as it affected the musicians it purported to serve. They weren't about to be put out to pasture or left to paint the roof. While aging rock stars at play in any field make easy targets for mockery or even pathos, to do so risked missing a great resource: the voice of hard-earned wisdom. "There's a great saying: 'Experience grinds the lens through which we perceive reality,'" said Dave Stewart, cofounder of the Eurythmics. "Once you open your lens wider and wider, you start realizing there's a whole massive world of art forms, and there's a whole massive world of people that can be part of it. That's what I'm trying to say as I'm whistling myself through the Internet."

Or, as Ice-T put it, "Most of the [younger] artists don't really know what the fuck they're talking about! They're just so happy to have a record deal, they don't know. You have to be an artist that's been through the entire mill. I've fuckin' been hit with every type of thing that the record companies have, from being signed and loved, to wantin' to be dropped, to being pushed over the edge, so I'm a veteran of the recording war." For those with a comfortable living, or at least a name to trade on, like Ice-T, Stewart, and especially Bowie, the Net was a fascinating experiment in development, an area to devote their time to and an arena where they were given respect that didn't always come easily in the charts-driven world of pop music. It could even be profitable. As The Byrds' Roger McGuinn testified before Congress, the popularity gained by having his songs distributed on the Net meant a revival of his career.

It may not have been musicians who built the technology in use, but the twin forces of necessity and curiosity pushed them to see what they could make of the Internet. As a force for personal empowerment and communication, the Net compelled musicians and audience to confront and deal with one another as never before. For bands like Metallica that felt ripped off by listeners who were newly empowered to make copies of the group's music, the meeting was not so nice. For others like David Bowie, who turned some of his fan base into paying customers for BowieNet, his Internet service provider-cum–fan site, it was a boon. For the Beastie Boys, it meant recruiting a fan of their music to be an active collaborator.

*   *   *

In 1992, as Web protocols were just freshly crafted, an Indiana University computer science student, Ian Rogers, was frustrated with the poor quality of Beastie Boys discographies appearing on Usenet news groups. "You'd go in there each week and every time you'd see a different discography and they were all wrong," said Rogers, who had the idea of taking the best ones and putting them on the Web as an accurate, growing compilation. "I just got kind of obsessed by it, as I often do, in my firm belief that anything worth doing is worth overdoing."

Rogers began to compile everything, putting up pictures and articles. As one of the first music Web sites, Rogers's project garnered a lot of visitors, and a lot of attention. Inevitably, word got back to Beasties management, who gave Rogers a call. Rogers was nervous. "I thought, Oh great, they're going to shut this thing down, because I've got so many scanned photos and articles, but they're like 'no, this is super cool, and we'll send you more shit.'" Soon Rogers received huge packages of Beasties releases and photos that he added to the site.

When the band came through Indiana as part of the 1994 Lollapalooza tour, Rogers was invited to the show to meet them. Because he thought the manager was just trying to be nice to him, and because he wasn't interested in the huge venue, Rogers declined. He then got another call not only imploring him to attend, but also asking if he could show the Web site to the band. He decided to go, and he and the group hit it off famously.

According to Rogers, the Beasties weren't interested in his site necessarily to promote the band, but because Mike Diamond and Adam Yauch had various outside interests and ventures that they were hoping to market inexpensively. "Mike had [the magazine] *Grand Royal* at the time, and Yauch had [the charity organization] Milarepa just starting . . . . That's the vision that bands are starting to get now: taking their fan base and building it into something more, and we were doing that then."

The idea of connecting with fans, nurturing the community, and pinpointing marketing efforts to a receptive core perfectly suited the Internet. The Beasties discussed the possibilities with Rogers. "We went through a whole plan of what we might do," he said. That plan included directly marketing the upcoming album *Hello Nasty* to the fans who frequented the Web site. "Capitol was smart enough to want to use the Internet as a main marketing tool. They said we should at least be getting those couple hundred thousand kids on the day of sale." The other questions were about how to use the band's Web site to keep fans happy. "We decided we could give them a lot." The group released its next video on the site, before it was released on MTV, as well as music before it went to radio.

The Beastie crew also came up with a way to mobilize their fans by putting together a street team of 200 kids. They sent out packages of promotional materials months before the record came out. "At first we'd send out stickers, and the ones that did cool shit with stickers got posters, and the ones that did cool shit with posters got T-shirts. We kept whittling it down, and by the end we were only sending out to like twenty kids around the country." One young New Yorker dressed up in a lab coat with "Hello Nasty, July 17th" painted on it and went to his local mall to hand out stickers. Impressed by his dedication, the band invited him out when they hit New York on their tour. "He was stoked," Rogers said.

In 1998, the group went on the road again, and Rogers went along with them again to post more photos and stories from the road. What really attracted attention was that Rogers started recording songs live from the soundboard, compressing them to MP3, and then posting them on the Web site for public consumption. The songs were a big hit with fans, but after a meeting between the Beasties and the label, the files were taken down from the site, prompting rumors that Capitol had handed the Beasties an ultimatum.

"That's what got us tons of press, but Capitol never asked us to pull those things down like the press reported time and time again," said Rogers. "That was just a great story: the band versus the label. The label did kind of question it, but we pulled them down ourselves because we only wanted them up there a couple weeks." For a long time, however, rumors were flying that Beastie Boys directly flaunted Capitol's wishes by pushing their own MP3s.

It wasn't just the fans and Capitol who were paying attention. The newly launched MP3.com was eager for big name content, to legitimize the format and generate traffic. Michael Robertson must have thought the Beasties were just the ticket, because his site began serving up copies of the Beasties' songs from its own pages, which came as a shock to Rogers and the Boys. Rogers noticed what had happened when he checked the Web site while on the road and was struck by the audacity.

"Those motherfuckers stole my song!" he said. He quickly e-mailed Robertson threatening letters, but finally relented to his request to leave the songs on the MP3.com site. In return, Robertson would save and forward the e-mail addresses of downloading fans. "They said they'd collect the e-mail addresses, but they never did give them to us," said Rogers. "It was awful. I did get a bunch of them months and months after I threatened them. I was writing to Michael Robertson personally, because he's the one I made the deal with, and I think he just had one of his technical guys give me some random 75,000 e-mail addresses."

Rogers was obviously proud of what he was able to do promoting the band, but was uncomfortable with being made to fit someone else's—usually a reporter's—ideology. "We were the first ones to put live MP3s on the Web site, before Napster or any of the MP3 wave. But the way the press put it was so weird, like we were 'joining the MP3 revolution.' For the Beastie Boys it's always been about how do you reach your fans. They were never supporting MP3 or not supporting MP3. At the time that was the way to reach the fans with music."

*   *   *

If the Beasties were first to use MP3s to promote their new music, veterans before them dabbled extensively in technology. Todd Rundgren, a psychedelic pop star and big-time record producer from a tender age, mixed it up with new computer and Internet technologies before almost any other star of his stature. In 1972, when Rundgren was twenty-four, *Rolling Stone* dubbed him "the all-around rock and roll whiz kid" after he had produced albums by The Band and Badfinger. He went on to not only have an influential career as a musician, but also to help artists as important and diverse as Patti Smith, the New York Dolls, and Meat Loaf achieve their vinyl masterpieces.

In the late '80s, Rundgren started to get involved in designing software and became a hero to hip budding Silicon Valley workers. His interactive music CD-ROM was one of the first works to take that format seriously, even though his idea—that listeners couldn't wait to remix the songs he put out—was probably misguided. The interactive mini-studio built into the program left many fans uninspired. By the time he hit his fifties, Rundgren once again proved himself several steps ahead of the rest of the world, by establishing a service to let fans subscribe directly to artists.

Dubbed PatroNet, Rundgren's subscription model let fans pick one of several tiers of support, which would give them the right to download his works, or receive shipments of his CDs in the mail, at a frequency suited to Rundgren's schedule, not a label's. Though PatroNet used unprotected MP3s, Rundgren said in a Yahoo chat in 1998 that he reserved the right to change the format if he felt like it. At a speech for the Webnoize convention that same year, he acknowledged that it was hard to make a case for ownership of songs when so much of popular music demanded the familiarity that could only come from freely borrowing ideas. "The demand for copyright protection means that (artists) are uncreative and afraid this is going to be the last song they'll ever write. It wouldn't be commercial if they didn't steal it from someone else," he said. He would later take a much more copyright-friendly stance as song trading on the Internet increased. Rundgren threatened to monitor songs on Napster and suspend the subscription of any PatroNet user giving away his music.

With the subscription service, Rundgren's objective was mainly to craft a more natural relationship among artist, audience, and the production of music. "I've grown through a lot of these eras," he said. "When I was really young there were no LPs at all. The first LPs you saw was when they invented the stereo and they wanted to demonstrate the fancy stereo effects. Most records had one song on them. A songwriter came up with a song for an artist, and everyone said, 'yeah I think it's about time that this artist put out a song,' they came up with a usually Spartan budget to put it together, and they did it in three hours. And if the artist did enough of those that went down well enough with the audience, they put that out as an album; that's what an album was, a collection of musical snapshots. You made music all the time; you didn't carve out a year to record an album. Or you didn't wait and wait and wait and then do it all in one spurt, and then wait and wait and wait. There have been artists that have adhered to that [original] dynamic even though the industry is geared another way. For instance, Elvis Costello will just make music all the time, and anytime he wants to get in a studio he'll just get in a studio.

"The problem is that in this day and age it's so expensive to manufacture and promote records that you are encouraged to do that lopsided thing. It's allowed me to get back into 'what do I want to do now,' not 'what do I think will make sense two years from now when the record's finished and comes out.' Or what is it that I would do naturally that wouldn't work in a record context. When you do a record it almost always is built around some stylistic or sonic concept that makes it all hang together. It's not necessary any longer to think in that hour-long concept. Now I can do anything. In the course of a natural musical flow in which people are getting music every eight weeks, or once a month, it's just a pleasant surprise. Anything I make I just put it up and say 'take it or leave it.'"

While the service did not get many rave reviews, or other artists, for that matter, the model provided inspiration for what was shaping up to be the music industry's next big stage. By mid-2000, the labels as well as MP3.com and Emusic had announced their own subscription services, and Jim Griffin spread the idea at speaking engagements and on mailing lists. Rundgren was also having fun trying to define and defend his role as cultural provocateur.

"An entertainer has to essentially satisfy the audience; an artist sometimes is required to torture the audience," he postulated. "Those are two different approaches to what you deliver, and whether you craft a subscription or some other product that you're going to offer, you better base it on something that you know you can deliver. Most people who subscribe to me know that there's an artistic component to what I do, which means that the agenda is not always to satisfy the audience but to raise new questions or push the parameters."

*   *   *

While established musicians with big names and a modicum of fans can experiment within and without record label structures, by 1999 there were still no unsigned bands that had used the Internet to push their music and achieve stardom, in the Madonna, Rolling Stones, or even Oasis meaning of the word. Two brothers who came close to tasting the first blush of fame were the Chicago rappers who made up La Junta, a group that learned firsthand that the new Web boss can be as fickle and full of letdowns as the old boss.

Xavier "X-Man" Nogueras started La Junta with his younger brother Jose, or "Grimlock," in 1998, when Xavier was 26 and Jose 22. The brothers, of Puerto Rican descent, grew up and lived in Chicago's Humboldt Park, an area known for a high rate of poverty as well as gang crime. While working a community activist job that followed in the footsteps of an older bother, Xavier also learned to use his computer and electronic instruments to make music that was heavily inspired by German techno pioneers Kraftwerk, with an added heavy edge that made it great for break dancing. Because his music was completely digital, with only the vocals ever existing outside of the closed loop of computer-based recording system and samplers, Xavier's older brother Miguel suggested that online distribution was the perfect way to reach a wider audience.

"He thought it made sense," said Xavier, "because the type of music we do is tied into technology, and we rap a lot about technology—remember, in the early days of hip-hop and break dancing people were using instruments and technology like nobody else was—they were actually innovators in technology."

In early 1999, when Miguel, who worked as a computer consultant, showed them an article about Michael Robertson and MP3.com, La Junta decided to put their music up on the site. They soon discovered that simply posting it wasn't enough. Their music wasn't going to find an audience on its own, and if they wanted an audience, they realized that they had to build it by themselves. Thankfully, Xavier was not only resourceful, he had also developed a knack for organizing communities. "For some reason we just figured out how to do the type of street marketing that we do in the 'hood. We were able to do it on the Internet and master it, and that's when we really blew up."

What the group soon mastered was a form of online street marketing emulating the industry practice of "sniping." On the street, sniping means putting up band stickers and information, and verbally spreading the hype about a group. "We did sniping on the Internet—we went to sites and hit them up with logos and stuff like that. People always focus in on the big sites, but we worked hard on getting personal homepages to put our logo up; building relationships." AOL chat rooms, they found, made the perfect arena for this type of relationship building, and word about the band began to snowball. By the time La Junta had perfected their online marketing skills, they quickly roped in friends, and even some interns, to keep things rolling forward.

MP3.com couldn't help but notice. Gearing up for an IPO later that year, and aching to establish itself as a genuine player in the music business, the company was tired of being perceived as a wasteland of indistinguishable garage bands. The notion of being a launching pad for a previously unknown group was an attractive prospect. Robertson and company agreed to help the band land a big-label record deal and brought in Ken Hertz, the entertainment lawyer.

Unfortunately, the meetings never quite gelled for the band, and despite what felt like a promising introduction to Hertz, Xavier thought he never seemed to follow up on the interest that "ten differ-ent labels" showed in his group. After complaints from the band, Hertz ducked out, explaining that he probably didn't have enough time to help them. That put Xavier on the defensive. At the same time, MP3.com secured a song from Ice-T in exchange for some MP3.com stock, hoping the song would help establish the company's rap cred. But despite the fame and the stock, Ice-T's song didn't seem to be overtaking La Junta in the number one spot on the site's rap charts. At least until what Xavier suspected was tampering. He called to complain, and then later that day La Junta's song was back at num-ber one. "It was so obvious that someone had manually done that . . . . The day after that Ice-T wasn't on the chart anymore. That was the beginning of the end," Xavier said.

"That was a bad experience, because we tasted stardom—we were on CNN, we had Will Smith's lawyer—and they just fucking dumped us after their IPO. I regret not suing them. In fact Paradise, the guy in charge of the hip-hop from MP3.com, actually came to see us, be-cause they thought we were going to sue them." While not exactly clear on the grounds for a case, Xavier believed that such a suit would have damaged the MP3.com IPO, which the site couldn't allow. Counting his blessings, while he still harbored some bad feelings, he admitted that "MP3.com made us."

MP3.com's publicist at the time, Hal Bringman, who was, along with his partner Phil McGovern, among those excited about La Junta's potential, agreed that the focus at the company drastically shifted. "The only concern in the period leading up to the IPO was the IPO itself, so that they didn't have time for the guys in La Junta," Bringman said. McGovern went further, asserting that a suit might actually have been possible and might have been particularly damag-ing given the timing. "It would have been very interesting," he said.

After La Junta stopped putting all their hopes in the MP3.com bas-ket, Xavier said they "found out that there was a whole other world out there for the MP3 format." The group posted its songs to sites in France, Germany, and Japan, where their songs caught on and rose to the top of the online charts. Fan clubs started sprouting up in places as unlikely as Estonia. In fall of 2000, the band planned to tour Germany, sponsored by a promoter who was impressed with seeing them on the charts of his country's besonic.com music Web site for so long.

"We might not have gotten that big record deal, but I think we did something even more important, more realistic: we have a successful career because of the Internet," said Xavier. The two were in demand at conferences all over the Midwest, explaining to other bands how to use Internet communities to spread their works. "We did a music seminar in Chicago showing people how they can access and put their hip-hop music online. The economy's not an excuse either, because if you can't afford a computer, there's one in the public library. So we went from being cyberstars to being ambassadors for groups to the Internet, and that made us popular with bands in the area."

They've also used their community service connections to secure funding for a neighborhood technology center, complete with digital recording and video studios, and a digital marketing suite, so that others can duplicate their efforts.

*   *   *

Although the Net hasn't yet become a replacement for the usual label-generated star-maker machinery, unsigned artists have hopes that the medium might develop in that direction. Even more than MP3.com, Garageband.com was a site depending on building the impression that it would help break artists from unknowns into the big time. Co-founded by Jerry Harrison, the Talking Heads bassist and former Modern Lover, the site sought to supplant traditional A&R discovery by letting bands and interested fans listen and vote for each other. Voters were not told the names of the band playing the tracks they randomly voted on, so band reputation counted for nothing. After the end of the several-month voting period, a winning group or performer would be chosen and awarded a $250,000 recording contract. While not exactly revolutionary, the process did seem to nicely democratize a system too often fraught with shady dealings. An advisory board headed by Sir George Martin of Beatles fame was rounded out with notables such as Brian Eno and Peter Gabriel's producer Steve Lilly-white.

The four members of Monovox had been playing together for the six years since their junior year in high school when they decided to try out Garageband. While the band started in a small town in rural Wisconsin, where they "had nothing better to do than play rock and roll for our friends and act like a bunch of drunken, pot-smokin' prima donnas," singer Anthony Shaw said that after a year of college, the foursome moved to Chicago to live together and continue their nonstop practicing. They hooked up with a manager and recorded an EP in the home of one of the Smashing Pumpkins.

While the group had messed around online for some time, the boys never took the Net all that seriously. Then MP3s came along, "and everything changed," said Shaw. Although not excited about the for-mat's sound quality, the group was thrilled to be able to send away limitless samples to fans, friends, and music reps. They remained skeptical about any kind of large-scale notoriety developing as a result of the Internet, especially since it was nearly impossible for an un-known band to find an online audience. But they turned into believers when, in 1999, Garageband.com started attracting visitors for them from across the globe. "Before we uploaded our tracks to the site, we had been receiving the majority of our hits from servers in Madison and Milwaukee. During the February Final Countdown, we began re-ceiving warm hello's from visitors in Oslo, London, and even Ha-vana." Their music convinced the listeners on the site, and the band earned the $250,000 contract. After Monovox traveled to San Fran-cisco to record, their album was set to come out in 2001. The world would find out if this was indeed the meritocratic replacement for the traditional sleazy rise to fame that most stars are still forced to make.

*   *   *

Alanis Morissette, hardly one in need of a record deal, is another artist who has benefited handsomely from her association with Internet

music. Even so, a year before 1999 she probably wouldn't have imagined herself raking in a fortune from Internet stock. The Canadian
singer with a fiery attitude had rocked the charts in 1995 with her an-
themic hell-hath-no-fury rebuke, "You Oughta Know," the single that
pushed her album, *Jagged Little Pill* to number 10 on *Billboard* charts,
where it found a home for years, eventually selling more than 16 million copies. Her career up to that point involved many dramatic ups
and downs, including being signed to MCA records at age 12, followed by teenage entanglements with much older TV stars, and touring dates supporting the frequently maligned rapper Vanilla Ice. Despite the massive variety in her life, becoming an Internet power
player seemed unlikely.

But Morissette had the fortune to engage Ken Hertz as her lawyer
and adviser. In the music industry, lawyers tend to occupy positions of
importance outweighing personal managers. The right attorney will
be abreast of industry-wide developments, keep a finger on the major
deals, and will have personal relationships with all the right players.
Having a larger number of clients tends to give the lawyer that much
more power. Hertz and his partner Fred Goldring, of the Beverly Hills
firm Hansen, Jacobson, Teller & Hoberman, had these in spades, and
the strength of their clientele to match.

Hertz had followed the development of the players and firms involved with online music with great interest. He was a speaker and a
moderator at the first MP3 Summit and made a conscious effort to
promote himself and Goldring as players within the newly developing
space, for a short time representing MP3.com. When music label
honchos and tech industry figures debated issues of the day at the
many Net conferences that were sprouting like mushrooms after a
summer rain, Hertz seemed ever ready to chime in with the perspective of the musician, or at least the perspective of one building lucrative careers for musicians. Within the industry, Hertz had a reputation as a killer negotiator and dealmaker. By default, it often fell on
him to explain the new world of opportunities to his roster of stars.

"It's part of my job to educate them if they ask me," Hertz said,
"and it's certainly my job to educate them if they need to understand
what it is that they're doing. I don't make decisions for my clients; all

I can do is to give them the information and try to be as objective as possible and explain to them what the risks and the rewards can be." Hertz and Goldring looked hard to identify ways to push the limits of the opportunities that were developing. "What we try to do is to look for ways that artists can define themselves through one of these kinds of promotional activities. Let's be fair: these events can either be interpreted as important statements about where connectivity is likely to take the entertainment industry, or they can be perceived as publicity stunts, and if they're just stunt marketing it becomes progressively more difficult to come up with a good enough stunt that's going to turn enough heads or raise any eyebrows. How often can you do something that no one's ever done before?"

That opportunity came in early 1999. As the media world looked jealously at the fortunes being made by the initial stock offerings of Internet-based companies, it was natural that the shrewd would try to get in on some of that action, and Hertz was certainly shrewd. In 1999, MP3.com was almost completely filled with bands that existed outside the label system. Few had much money, so the music they offered was usually less polished, and because none had anything matching the publicity budgets that even a mid-sized label would offer, almost none of the bands had any public recognition.

As Michael Robertson guided MP3.com towards its IPO, he wanted desperately to associate with big-name artists. Morissette, meanwhile, was in the midst of booking a tour to support *Supposed Former Infatuation Junkie*, her follow-up record, and from most perspectives a stronger, more mature work. As is often the case, the new album would struggle to live up to the commercial promise of her big hit. Possibly inspired by Hertz's close association with MP3.com (though he declines to take credit), Morissette's manager, Scott Welch, at the Atlas/Third Rail agency, approached Robertson with a deal. MP3.com would join Best Buy as sponsors of Morissette's tour, as well as issue stock options to Morissette. In return, Robertson was hoping that he would finally have a big name artist's validation of the format his company was built on. It didn't quite work out that way. In order to avoid damaging her relationship with her label, Madonna's Maverick Records, Morissette would only allow Robertson to stream one song. For that she would walk away with options for over 300,000 shares, at the low exercise price of thirty-three cents per share. And from all indications, the IPO was shaping up to be a winner.

"It wasn't my decision; it wasn't my idea," offered Hertz. "It was her manager's idea, I simply made the introduction—and I didn't even negotiate the deal. Most people aren't aware of that. I simply made the introductions and then helped clear the road at the record label."

Aside from the cash that the deal offered, Hertz said that the association with MP3.com was perfect for boosting Morissette's image as well as her tour. "Cash was something they didn't have, and the tour sponsorship was valuable not just because of the upside it created for her financially, but because of the identity it created for her. Alanis I think always likes to be a little further out on the edge in terms of her thinking, whether it's spiritual thinking, commercial thinking, professional thinking, creative thinking, or what have you. It was an opportunity for her to define herself to her audience."

For Hertz, the deal proved that the artist's name and music were still valuable properties, which might bode well for future deals. "It was a watershed event that helped define where this stuff was going. What was important about it was that it was an artist taking their career into their own hands in a new way."

By the time her year of waiting to exercise her stock options was over, Morissette filed to sell 100,000 shares, from which, Reuters reported, she expected to clear $1,000,000.

Robertson was left to brood over giving away so much and getting back so little. For a man whom David Weekly characterized as "hungry for money like a leech for blood," getting ripped off had to smart, and that ugly side began to surface more frequently. Bringman recalled Robertson's blustery attempt to cover the sinking suspicion that he might have been had. "She only gave him one little stream!" said Bringman. "That was really an amazing coup for Ken Hertz."

Robertson could not spend much time in reflection, however; he had something much bigger on his plate. MP3.com's IPO was scheduled for July, and the company was in its quiet period. For Hal Bringman, the subdued activity during this time was the beginning of his departure from the company. But luckily for all, the PR machine was rolling along with little help. In fact, it could be argued that if there had been more public speaking, harm might have come from further clarifications that MP3.com did not actually invent this new technology that everyone was suddenly hearing so much about.

The little matter of a quiet period did not stop Robertson from orchestrating PR events, or reaping the benefit of stories in the press, or timing the second MP3 Summit to occur in June, just weeks before the IPO. Despite Universal president Larry Kenswil's speech in which he laughably stated that the Internet simply wouldn't be able to handle the amount of data transfer necessary to sustain music commerce on the scale of current CD distribution, most of the summit that year was fuel for the rising fire of MP3.com brand recognition. Every product announcement or kid with a logo dyed and shaved in his scalp just added to the excitement that was growing, and the sentiment that this could well be the biggest thing to ever hit the Net. Even *Wired* magazine emblazoned its August cover with the bold cry "I want my MP3!"

Tech watchers would have to have been blind to miss the growing frenzy. To not invest would have been to risk being forever sorry. This was also the chance for artists far from Morissette's level to profit from the lure of instant riches. To Robertson's credit, all MP3.com artists were allowed to purchase up to 500 shares in the company; while some complained that the number was small, the offer was a decent show of good faith.

Still, there was shock at the MP3.com offering, when it finally transpired on July 2. The stock opened at $28 a share and rose quickly to $63, giving the company a short-lived valuation of $6.9 billion, a figure that was, as News.com pointed out that day, just over EMI's valuation of $6.4 billion. But the elation was tempered with nervousness. The same News.com story featured Forrester Research analyst Mark Hardie putting a damper on the sound of popping corks. "MP3.com [shares are] going to be worth less than $6 in six months," he speculated. "It's going to go out huge and then go through the floor. MP3.com is just not going to be a major player under their current model."

Other companies also benefited from the exuberance that propelled the MP3.com stock, chiefly Liquid Audio. The competitor, which had grown increasingly hostile towards Robertson's philosophy, saw its shares rise on opening day, July 9, from $15 to $36.56, giving Gerry Kearby's protection- and commerce-oriented company a market value of $658.7 million.

If Morissette took home a great amount of cash for very little actual substance, many were saying the same thing about Robertson. Bringman saw firsthand that "there was no vision after the IPO. Michael Robertson, when they asked him what kind of business he was in, said they were in the IPO business." How could the IPO business compete with the record industry?

5

The
Established Order

The Recording Industry Association of America, formed in 1952, represents the big five labels in the United States and watches out for their common interests: lobbying Congress to pass favorable laws and taking on their adversaries, usually in court. For most of the 1990s, and especially as issues on the Web such as file trading began to heat up, the labels were happy to let the association take care of the messy work and generally cooled their heels—hoping that a playing field would emerge, that, if it wasn't exactly level, would at least be tilted their way. That made it easy for the online world to mentally group the major labels into one multiheaded behemoth. But record labels as a rule work independently of each other. Virgin employees, for instance, are known to righteously assert that a distinctly smart, modern feeling exists at their label, which they consider a downright superior enterprise to EMI, the parent that bought them in 1992. When companies are separate, the competition can get brutal. In the famously chronicled "Walter's War" staged by CBS head Walter Yetznikoff against Warner Bros. in the late '70s, Yetznikoff went so far as to paint signs saying "Fuck Warner" and hand out combat boots to his "army" of workers at the CBS records convention. The situation has been complicated by the fear of the Internet as a greater enemy, but the competition has not withered.

"There's no mutual aid society," affirmed Ted Cohen, formerly of Warner and now vice president of interactive media at EMI. He pointed out that all of the labels do their own deals, and though the Internet was one area where the labels had tried to stick together, even there all sides were busy hatching their own plans. "Yes, the RIAA is an overall organization that tries to help with things that are industry agendas, but the intercompany competition is very fierce," Cohen said. "It's not five companies working in lockstep."

Instead the industry is a network of acquired and merged entities that are each a shifting piece in the wealthy mosaic of communications and entertainment conglomerates. Universal Music Group, the world's largest music company, changed owners in 2000, as its owner Seagram was sold to French media giant Vivendi, which quickly changed its name to Vivendi Universal. The corporation consists of record labels Interscope, Geffen, A&M, MCA Records, Polygram, Universal Motown Records Group, Island, Def Jam, MCA Nashville, Mercury, Verve, and Universal Classics Group, among others. Universal Vivendi also owns the French film and TV company Canal+, Universal Studios, Universal Pictures, and Havas Press, as well as more than 25 million shares in AOL Time Warner.

The Bertelsmann Music Group (BMG) is also part of an enormous enterprise, Bertelsmann AG, a German-based multinational with annual revenues of $17.6 billion. BMG Entertainment is the parent company to record labels RCA, Arista, and Ariola, among others, with a reported revenue of $4.7 billion in the 1999–2000 fiscal year. BMG also owns one of the world's largest music publishing companies, one of the world's leading compact disc and cassette manufacturing companies, and the world's largest record clubs, BMG Music Service, which runs BMGMusicService.com, which takes the 12-albums-for-the-price-of–1 model into the Internet frontier. In the United

States, Bertelsmann owns publishing giant Random House Inc. and Gruner + Jahr magazine publishers, including *McCall's*, *Parents*, *Family Circle* and *YM* magazines. In Europe it has even bigger holdings, including a heap of TV networks such as English Channel 5, French Fun TV, M6, and Multivision; four TV stations in the Netherlands, and five in Germany. It owns the German magazines *Der Spiegel*, *Geo*, *Stern*, and a host of others. Online it has at least 50 percent of the shares of AOL Europe, Germany, France, and Australia and of Lycos Europe and all of the online retailer CDNow.

Sony Music became a huge label force in the eighties when it acquired CBS Records and Columbia. Other Sony labels include Epic, 550 Music, Crave, Tri-Star Music, and Relativity. Big-name Sony acts include Jennifer Lopez, Bruce Springsteen, Offspring, Bob Dylan, and Barbra Streisand. Sony sold about $6 billion in the 1999 fiscal year, while that same year Sony Electronics had record sales of about $12.2 billion. As an empire based at its heart on the development of smart technology at the service of personal experience, Sony might be expected to take to online music with gusto. After all, the Walkman player was not only revolutionary in the way it let people integrate music into their lives and many environments, it was also a huge cause for much home taping. And as a defendant in the case that established the consumer's right to videotape television shows, Sony was expected by many to have some special sympathy for, or at least insight into, the plight of online music. It may have, but that didn't make it move noticeably faster than the rest.

The English company EMI was a hotly coveted property during the rise of online music, as it prepared to be taken over by successive suitors. The marriage with Time Warner was all but set when objections by European Community regulators nixed the union because of monopoly concerns, which were especially keen given the ongoing development of an online music infrastructure. EMI heads quite a household itself, with Richard Branson's Virgin records, Capitol, and Chrysalis all part of the family. The Beatles, Lenny Kravitz, and Garth Brooks helped the company rake in over $3.5 billion in 2000. Still reeling from being kept apart from Time Warner, EMI found itself entertaining offers from Bertelsmann.

When AOL took over and merged with Time Warner, it was viewed as a trophy of the Internet's triumph over old media—or as a fluke of a hyper-inflated tech stock that allowed the Virginia-based company to absorb the massive New York conglomerate. In 2000, the ramifications of a technology-centered ownership had only just begun. With a group that included CNN, Time Life Books, HBO, Warner Bros. films, and America Online companies like Winamp, the company, one could argue, was less international than the others and more rooted in its huge business in America. The labels that fell under Warner were impressive: Atlantic, Elektra, Warner Brothers, and Reprise among them. Red Hot Chili Peppers, Faith Hill, Frank Sinatra, The Doors, and Led Zeppelin were some of those companies' top hit makers.

Despite Cohen's confirmation that the five big record labels are very independent, throughout the 1990s, when it came to the Internet, the labels cooperated more than usual. The majors had agreed to drag their heels at every possible step when it came to the Net. It was unproven, and, especially for those invested in the machinery of delivery, it seemed dangerous. So they focused on piracy with their watchdog the RIAA. Being essentially a legal group, RIAA's concentration was on litigating and lawmaking, rather than research or development that might create new models. Preserving the status quo of the nondigital world was the goal, unless expanding members' rights was an option.

Until mid-decade, the Internet held little interest for the association. While it could foresee some potential for making money, before MP3.com—and well before Napster—the investment in the electronic home of nerds and hackers seemed like a money pit, while copyright violations there posed minimal mainstream threat. In the late 1990s, however, the association's work took a dramatic turn toward policing the online world. But by the time association noticed what was happening, the power and rate of change had upset the status quo. "Staying ahead of technologically advanced pirates presents a greater challenge than ever before," said Steve D'Onofrio, RIAA executive vice president and director of antipiracy, in a prepared statement in 1997. "While we work to protect the artists, record companies and everyone else involved in the creative process, we remain committed to allocating the resources to educate Internet users. We will also continue to establish critical legal precedents before the technologies advance to the point that large-scale online piracy runs rampant." Or so he hoped.

Record labels and band management all pitched in to swat the breeding online menace. The danger those days was chiefly from online shrines built by overzealous fans or from trading areas that offered songs for download—activities with strictly geek appeal at the time. The second prospect was a little slippery, but since fan sites made no effort to hide—they were aching to spread to the word— these were the first to come under the gun.

Dealings with Oasis fans typified the shut-them-all-down approach. In May 1997, Sarah Frederikson, an employee of the band's management in charge of the official Oasis home page, sent an e-mail to nearly all Oasis fan sites, insisting that they take down all copyrighted materials: photos, song clips, and lyrics, or face prosecution. The letter was evidently following a lead by Sony, though Oasis management would later claim full responsibility. A small carrot was dangled: Those who cooperated would be included in the official Oasis "fan page links" section. Otherwise, the letter said, "We will be forced to take appropriate action with those who do not change their sites to reflect these policies." Failure to comply with the law, it said, would result in legal action. A group calling itself the Oasis Webmasters for Internet Freedom was formed, insisting that their inclusion of copyrighted materials fell under the provisions of fair use. By the time a thirty-day deadline had arrived, though, the vast majority of fan pages had closed, which nearly ended the controversy. The same year, Sony records itself shut down a fan site dedicated to Oasis. An English fan, Derek Gorman, had been serving up several clips of songs from an upcoming Oasis album, which he'd downloaded from an official Sony site in Brazil. While the clips were not full-length songs, and served to whet appetites for more music, Sony wanted full control and contacted Gorman's service provider, which turned off the offending site.

After signing an agreement with Sony attorneys, Gorman had his site restored.

This was the typical pattern for the labels, and it left a long trail of disillusioned, embittered online fans. Their first contact with the music industry—which made its billions nurturing devotion and involvement—was one of threats, finger pointing, and legal action.

If it has wavered in its excitement about the Internet as an entertainment vehicle, the entertainment industry has been steadfast in its wariness of Internet culture. The enormous free-for-all, where information exists to be absorbed, processed, and appropriated by all, is threatening to those who see their business as one of controlling properties. When *Star Trek* fans, for example, started getting a little too enthusiastic and taking too many liberties with their adoptions on Web sites, they were swiftly asked to cease. To be fair, the persistent vigilance is necessitated by copyright law itself, which works in a use-it-or-lose-it way: those who don't exercise their rights against small infringements lose them against future, larger ones. Still, after all, where would *Star Trek* be now if it weren't for an incredibly active legion of fans and their willingness to step way over the boundaries of standard cultural consumption?

*   *   *

Fan shrines, it turns out, were small game. By 1997, sites such as David Weekly's were on the rise, powerful amateur trading posts that offered music to college students who had discovered the wonders of high-speed desktop Net service, especially when their friends were also connected. Then they discovered MP3s. An industry press release boasted of the successes it was having as a policeman. "In 1997, the RIAA sent notification regarding hundreds of Internet sites informing them that they were infringing member companies' rights. The overwhelming majority were promptly shut down. The few remaining sites are seeking proper licensing or removing unlicensed recordings. The majority of the sites that came down were using MP3 technology, an advanced compression technology that allows users to download, and in some cases, upload hundreds of full-length, near CD-quality sound recordings, without the permission of the copyright holder."

A new enemy demanded a new general. At the time these ominous press releases were made, the RIAA was looking for someone capable of waging a fierce war against the massive change and disruption occurring because of the Internet. But there was a catch: a campaign of action to house-train the Internet was likely to mean more public exposure than the association had ever had, and the new spokesperson needed a warm touch and a disarming presence. The association got that person with Hilary Rosen. A former representative of songwriters, Rosen was not only skilled in litigation but was also a persuasive lobbyist and a friendly, if lawyerly, voice. Already a veteran of the RIAA, having joined in 1987, Rosen had previously operated a consulting firm and honed her lobbying skills in Washington. In January of 1998, she became the president and CEO of the association.

By virtue of her timing, Rosen would play a role that was markedly different from that of any other chief of the association. She assumed the helm just as Internet-driven technologies were on a collision course with the heart of what the RIAA was trying to protect. Driving the litigation and the legislation that most affected these developing industries and cultures, when even the nation's tax laws were held at bay so that the Internet could grow unimpeded, was a brave move. Her position also made Rosen the bull's-eye on a legion of Internet users' mental dartboards. She would make light of her predicament, telling reporters, "The scrutiny is a lot brighter. We're out there in the sunshine, and it feels fine." Rosen would have had to have been tough indeed not to feel the pressure, however, and others in the industry often expressed their admiration for her fortitude, and in the same breath their sympathy for her plight at being so personally vulnerable to the strong wave of resentment that came in backlash to the RIAA's attempts to shut down Web sites and sue companies that helped users to get copyrighted songs. As the battle raged on, there would be continual rumors that Rosen was on the verge of resignation.

Rosen was no stranger to controversy, including personal attacks. When she and her lesbian partner adopted twins from a Texan mother, the religious Right in that state caught wind of the adoption and did its best to single out the family by writing letters to every member of the Texas legislature, objecting to Rosen and her partner, Elizabeth Birch, by name.

"Hilary and I have always had gay rights issues in the forefront of our lives, but we have never had anything cut as close to our souls as becoming parents," Birch, the director of the gay rights organization the Human Rights Campaign, told *The Advocate*. "The bonding process with your children is so deep that we would do anything to protect it from those who threaten it. What we did in adopting is a very private thing, and when the Right got hold of it, it felt very mean and personal." As it would when the RIAA entered the battle to separate Internet users, many of whom exhibit great senses of personal entitlement to their free boxes of music cookies.

Aside from leading the ill-considered charge to stop the Diamond Rio, among Rosen's first steps as CEO was to move quickly to support and push forward the negotiations involved in drafting the Digital Millennium Copyright Act, an act that would clarify issues of copyright in the digital realm and strengthen the laws protecting copyright holders.

Looking back from the year 2000, Rosen would characterize her efforts at the helm of the RIAA as answering the question: "How do we accelerate the legitimate music market online? Everything that we've done," Rosen said, "whether it's lawsuits, whether it's anti-piracy, whether it's technology standards, whether it's marketing and education—it has all been geared with that goal." Of course, Rosen's job was not just to make sure what happened online was legal, but rather to make sure that the RIAA's constituents continued to earn money and grow. Doing that, they seemed to feel, meant staying in charge. Anyone threatening the hegemony would meet fierce resistance.

Rather than tackling the record companies head on, Michael Robertson's MP3.com tried to spot areas of distribution that the majors had ignored and harnessed the power of the Internet in attempts to make these areas profitable. One of his first attempts was Digital Automatic Music, or DAM, by which MP3.com would press and mail CDs on the fly for any band posting songs on its site. While MP3.com would share in 50 percent of the profits, it asserted no claim on the music, and every band was free to opt out when it wanted. Of course, there was absolutely no promotion involved, and insiders like ex-Geffen technologist Jim Griffin laughed at suggestions that this was a serious option for musicians. The issue, according to Griffin, was simple: "What are you bringing to the party to help that artist? That's why people sign with big labels—they have the resources that are necessary. For all the criticism they might get, they do put a lot of money into the bands they sign. If you get signed by a major label, they're going to put six figures of money into you at the bare minimum, and that helps any business."

And without that money? "I think the odds of someone buying a record or dealing with a band they've never heard of is infinitesimally small," said Griffin. "This is sort of an incubator with very little resources for a band. They are willing to share those resources that they have, but those are relatively meager, even in the digital world."

Robertson, however, was thrilled with the implications of his new service and launched it with much fanfare, hoping to contrast MP3.com with the old-style music industry by pointing to other high-tech models. "What Dell did for the PC, we're doing for the CD. We're doing it direct: The CDs are produced and shipped to the buyers direct. We're doing just-in-time ordering: We actually produce the CD when it's ordered." The industry wasn't scared; most players had the same wizened stance as Griffin's and snickered at the idea of a naïf like Robertson taking stabs at modernizing an entrenched industry from outside its walls. But the fact that Robertson, like other young tech rebels, remained so far outside the music industry was to many a sign of the industry in crisis. Even workers within the industry who had any drive to modernize were ignored, their ideas withering on the vine. Griffin, in 2000, remembered the problem: "I would say it was '95 or '96 that everyone started jumping ship—and the fact that they did it so long ago and the industry is just now realizing it shows how deeply asleep they are."

While DAM was one, perhaps naïve, attempt, others followed. The rise of the swift, sometimes grassroots Internet music companies and communities was contrasted by a slow, dense industry that was simply complacent, when it wasn't fearful or bogged down by incredibly complex contracts. Jim Griffin elaborated on the latter, and suggested that the slowness of the dinosaurs contributed to the success of their more nimble adversaries.

"The record companies really blew it by not hiring the Weeklys, Lords, and Ian Clarkes," Griffin said. "In any other business these people would be working in-house. We'd be out recruiting them one after another, spending money. I think clearly this industry doesn't do that, and that's unfortunate." There was an upside, though, because a rejection of new blood with new ideas led to a vital industry outside of the entertainment industry, where the MP3.coms, Napsters, and Nullsofts were born. "So I thank God, really . . . because it enabled an empowerment outside of the traditional structures."

The higher one went in the label hierarchies, the stronger the resistance was; at the top, Griffin described the environment as "stifling." Although he loved working with the "fantastic" people at Geffen, after Universal began asserting its power, it became much less desirable to remain there. "That point arrived when I thought: 'It's time to leave, because David [Geffen]'s not here anymore, and the other executives are leaving, and if they're not around anymore this is not going to be a good place to work. We'll have to be working for those people across the hill who have proven they really don't get it.'"

Even when the people across the hill were excited by a technology, it was the wrong one. While Griffin helped to release the Aerosmith song online in early 1994, Geffen's parent, Universal, was telling him that the enhanced CD-ROM was "the future." That belief lasted as late as 1996. "You're thinking 'What's wrong with picture? This is a mistake.'" Back down a notch on the corporate pyramid, vision was still worth something: Geffen awarded Griffin a bonus in 1996 for steering the company away from CD-ROMs.

*   *   *

The Secure Digital Music Initiative was the music industry's main technical stab at dealing with the Napster problem on its own digital territory. The group was announced by the RIAA on December 15, 1998, and commenced work February 26, 1999. As luck would have it, the man who was hired to be executive director was Leonardo Chiariglione, a serious, sometimes blustering Italian engineer who was also head of the Motion Picture Experts Group, the organization that developed MP3. The organization grew to 180 member companies, a mixture of record labels, electronics manufacturers, and online ventures. The project's aim was to craft a set of standards that all sides agreed to, in order to protect online music from unauthorized duplication. While there was no exact timetable, the initiative was to consist of two phases. The first SDMI-compliant devices and programs would pretty much accept all files while recognizing built-in features like watermarks. In the second phase, if a song was detected as having been illegally copied, the device would refuse to play the song. It sounded simple enough, but with so many competing voices, all with veto power, very little happened. Cliques of engineers didn't mix well with boisterous record industry folks. But the initiative created a jet-set position in each company: to be equitable to such an international group of representatives, each bimonthly meeting was held in a different city, such as Tokyo, New York, or Florence. Though many entertainment expense accounts were reported, another standard file type to replace MP3 was never hatched.

By 1999, even Chiariglione was frustrated. In April, he delivered a speech that was reported in *Wired News* as being "stern, scolding" and painfully longwinded. Continually referring to himself in the third person, he said that "after fourteen months in charge of this body the executive director sees the future in a much less rosy way." He was disappointed that the different sides kept vetoing each other's schemes. "The executive director considers this behavior against the terms of participation, which explicitly say that the purpose of the SDMI specification is to enable multiple business models."

Like most observers (and, off the record, a good deal of the participants), David Weekly was skeptical. "The fact of the matter is, MP3 is here now. Yes, it is not as high quality. Yes, it has a reputation for piracy and illegal copying. But you know what? Tens of millions of consumers are using it today," he wrote in a March 1999 column. "It is too late for SDMI," he said, because even if SDMI were finalized in a year, the range of MP3 for digital audio encoding, distribution, and listening would "prove far more compelling to the consumer than an investment in new technology for the explicit purpose of restricting their access to music."

The recording industry was always looking for the right new technology, but it was continually stymied by a long tradition of iron-fist control. Even Rosen's RIAA wanted a legitimate music market online only if its constituents were clearly in charge. Whether by virtue of a noncooperative record industry, free options like MP3.com or later Napster, or simply the disinterest of the consumer, those online companies that tried to play ball with industry had a tough time. If Liquid Audio did what it could to gain record industry acceptance, Emusic stuck to its own terms, as it tried hard to own the online music retail space. Despite a scrupulously legal approach, because the company used unencrypted MP3s it was an industry pariah. Emusic's chairman, Bob Kohn, and its president and CEO, Gene Hoffman, first met when working for Pretty Good Privacy, a company that popularized encryption for a surprisingly receptive audience of Internet users. A record label concerned about an MP3 situation that it thought was spiraling out of control asked PGP to look into the possibilities of using encryption for online music.

After much deliberation, and despite an affinity for encryption that might have biased them the other way, Kohn and Hoffman came to believe that encryption was not going to work for music distribution. "Gene and Bob gave it some thought and concluded that [MP3 was] not a good application for security and encryption software, and that really there's nothing that can be done to protect the music," said Emusic spokesman Steve Curry.

Kohn had significant experience as an entertainment lawyer, and it was natural for him and Hoffman to brainstorm the online music phenomenon. They imagined a company with a relatively simple premise: sell music online just like a standard retail operation, but with digital goods. Song files would be offered for 99 cents, albums for $8.99. All songs were in the MP3 format, unhampered by any-one's encryption or protection scheme. The company launched as GoodNoise in 1998 and quickly changed its name to Emusic.

To the labels, which wanted to preserve their own distribution sys-tem, Emusic's concept was scary, and for the most part they chose not to cooperate. This meant that Emusic would focus on the indepen-dent labels, in order to build a stock of material that would form a convincing site. Blessed with plenty of funding, Emusic quickly as-sembled a team of industry dropouts and insiders who would try to convince record labels and select independent artists to sign with them for an exclusive five-year contract. To sweeten the deal they would throw in some cash. Though amounts like $40,000 didn't seem like much compared with Internet millionaires, for a basement-run label it could seem like a windfall.

Plenty of small labels were happy to sign over their Internet rights, at least for half a decade. Many criticized the company for becoming a one-shot sugar daddy to independent record labels, throwing cash at them for signing away their online rights. Emusic's offerings were shaping up, but unfortunately, its selection was only slightly more renowned than that of MP3.com. Artists such as Frank Black and They Might Be Giants were the company's biggest draws, though a deal with Epitaph in 1999 brought Emusic a popular selection of hardcore punk and perennial favorite Tom Waits.

While the company was indeed on top of the heap when it came to selling files online, the heap was proving to be a rather unimpressive one to rule. "You've got the fervent, hard core [saying] 'There's noth-ing you can do about it, music will be free,'" explained Emusic's Curry. "On the other side you've got the major labels and their camp saying 'No, we're going to add security and digital rights manage-ment to this music and watermarks to CDs to keep people from doing what they want to do, and keeping us in control.' What Emusic is say-ing is 'Look, there is an alternative, where fans can get the music, pay a flat low-cost fee, and collecting the music still feels free, but they get more out of it because labels and bands are involved.' And artists and labels can relax and know that they're going to be compensated for this." It sounded good in practice, though sales were not great, even as the company burned through cash. But the Internet economy was in full bloom, and the slow starts of others seemed like no deterrent to raising cash and starting new enterprises.

By 1999, in a field of "irrational exuberance," things were getting so full that newly arising companies began simply to seem like permutations of one another, each trying different combinations of strategies, hoping that a certain providential mixture would spark the right magic and set the form. There was excitement in the air, and money being thrown around. Former shoestring music conventions, such as North by Northwest in Portland, Oregon, were suddenly ground zero for an explosion of giveaways and general money frenzy let loose by the frothing music dot coms. Buses drove through the streets of Portland—and fleets of painted trucks in Austin for South by Southwest—proclaiming new startups, while swank parties were thrown featuring an overabundance of food, drink, and entertainment. It seemed as if the new online economy might let all players fulfill at least some of their fantasies about playing rock stars, even if it just meant getting drunk after hours and being driven home to a fancy hotel.

One of the biggest movers at the Portland convention was Palo Alto's Riffage, launched that year by Ken Wirt, then forty-seven, one of the honchos behind Diamond Rio's push. Riffage's main idea was to direct an appeal to unsigned acts, in hopes of building a sizable roster of songs, as well as boosting community. Of course this was straying directly into MP3.com's well-defined territory, but Riffage did have the advantage of appearing a little more sincere, as well as a little more into the music—one of the notoriously nonmusical Michael Robertson's vulnerable points. It was also Riffage's intention to maintain ties as close as possible to the street level of music consumption.

As some companies looked only ahead, trying to imagine the next wave of moneymaking and distribution, Riffage was fiercely setting up operations that were distinctly old school. A concert series was planned that would be filmed in coordination with the college-oriented Burly Bear cable network. *Riffage Live* aired across the country on cable and Internet, beginning in April 2000.

While other companies in San Francisco's exploding digital economy were content to snatch up old apartments or warehouses and convert them into offices, Riffage acquired a San Francisco institution to take a test dip into the offline world of concerts. The Great American Music Hall, a large and ornate concert palace, and former bordello, built just after the great earthquake in 1907, had hosted years of concerts by stars such as Duke Ellington, the Grateful Dead, and Johnny Cash. Riffage expected to follow the lead of New York's Knitting Factory. Both clubs held concerts in spaces equipped with the latest technical gear to make simultaneous music streaming not only reliable, but, for bands, more of a regular expectation for playing a show, like getting free drinks, guest passes, and a space to sell gear.

Wirt said that with the many additions to the company, it was "creating a very cost-effective music ecosystem" which could use its many different outlets to synergistically market and promote new acts, and then profit from their successes. The label would seek to sign roughly six new artists a year from Riffage. Those signed artists would be "partners" and split net sales of all albums. Riffage, like others, was betting that its strategy was the perfect combination of several business plans.

While the online libraries, communities, stores, and simple homepages reached a peak of frenzied growth, one company—Listen.com—attempted to rise above the fray to create a music portal. Cataloging and linking to an exhaustive amount of music on the Web provided the golden opportunity to become a niche version of Yahoo. The objective was encyclopedic, a competitor to the Ultimate Band List that would remain unapologeticly Web-based. This enormous project was pieced together by a team of reviewers and launched under the command of CEO Robert Reid, an Internet industry veteran and writer, with input from Carl Steadman, the self-proclaimed "Net star" who had scored a hit with the early Web sensation suck.com. Listen.com would be the biggest editorial effort in the world of music—print included.

The main difference between Listen and Artist Direct's Ultimate Band List was that Listen would limit itself strictly to music that was available online and would take an aggressively editorial approach.

Hipsters from San Francisco's rich supply were taken on to express their opinions about everything from Truckin' Songs to Ambient Breakbeat. In fact, one of the first and most critical efforts was to expand the range of style definitions to create a "genre tree" to accommodate the explosion of subcategories that was sweeping the music world. Rather than a roster of self-congratulatory management bios, the staff section of the Listen reserved boasting space for editors to share their hipster credentials, which were legion. So many editors played in local bands that the weekly paper *San Francisco Bay Guardian* ran a front-page story about the "music geeks" to whom Listen was a career dream come true. While professing an agnostic approach to legal issues, in practice almost all of the music Listen linked to was unquestionably legitimate. Most disputed trading made use of file-sharing programs such as Napster, and thus had no permanent address.

The industry took notice and as the incredible ongoing growth in online music raised the prospect of a label-less future, the industry finally began to invest heavily in online ventures—hedging its bets as much as providing real vision. In February 2000, a group of companies, including BMG, EMI, Warner, Universal, and Madonna's Maverick Records plunked down an undisclosed sum to invest in Listen, probably in the tens of millions, earning the upstart a much coveted seal of industry approval.

Ground was shifting for many pioneers of online music. Real reacted with full strength when it realized that it had completely misjudged the popularity of digital downloads. The ease of listening to MP3s had quickly improved, as companies like Winamp, Music-Match, and Sonique continued to refine their products, adding database management tools driven by the gargantuan libraries that devoted MP3heads assembled. In May 1999, the larger RealNetworks entered the downloadable song fray with the launch of its Real Jukebox, a player with strong organizing features and huge marketing muscle, as well as a built-in CD ripper that would automatically digitize one's music library—one disc at a time—when played on the computer. The Jukebox was a fully integrated component of a suite of audio visual players called the Real Entertainment Center.

The Internet land grab was in full swing and there was plenty of money to go around. If a company couldn't be first, becoming the biggest seemed like the next best thing. With the success of the MP3 format, large companies came knocking on the doors of the businesses that actually made MP3 players. Nullsoft, creator of Winamp, was one of the first to be approached. That the suitor was AOL came as a big surprise, with the aftershock being the weight of its knock. The initial $80 million offering probably would have convinced anyone else immediately; not so with the Nullsoft team. So AOL, knowing that it suffered from a coolness deficit, sent an emissary to Sedona, the recently acquired trophy boy Marc Andreesson, to close the deal.

Jeff Patterson and Rob Lord, both then on Justin Frankel's Nullsoft team, didn't beat around the bush. They asked Andreesson point blank why he sold Netscape to AOL. "It doesn't make sense, does it? No one using Netscape is going to want to use AOL, and no one on AOL is going to understand Netscape." Andreesson's answer, recalls Lord, was "Exactly. It's communities of interest." Andreesson made the case that users of the Net all had the same needs: they needed a browser; they needed a community; they needed to be able to chat; they needed to be able to instant message. They needed their information aggregated and packaged for them, and some people weren't going to do it under the brand of AOL, they were going to need the brand of Netscape, or Compuserve, and some of them needed the brand of Winamp.

"You guys are a growing community," he said. "And we're all about growing sticky communities." Everyone requires the same infrastructure, he explained, "we need big servers; lots of bandwidth; we need to make money and sell advertising." In a crowded field, a large, diverse firm such as AOL would be the ideal, if not only, way to survive and prosper. Nullsoft could continue to create its software and Web site to grow users and AOL would pick from its many brands the ideal partners to service. The speech was convincing.

On June 1, 1999, AOL announced that it would acquire Nullsoft, as well as the Internet radio company Spinner, for $400 million total. AOL president Bob Pittman picked up where Andreesson left off and said that combining Winamp and Spinner with the audience reach of its brands would lift online music to "the next level of popularity," which for AOL meant all over its network. "We plan to build downloadable music, Internet radio, and overall music features into each of our brands, as well as customize them for the audience and partners of each of our brands."

All of this legitimate activity was, if not exactly heartening to the recording industry powers that be, at least something that they could handle. They were even starting to get involved, to dispel any perceptions of technophobia. By the middle of 1999, the RIAA was trying to shift the online debate towards new opportunities. Hilary Rosen made several appearances in which she seemed to consciously downplay the threat of piracy, focusing instead on new opportunities and new strategies for the labels to pursue. In an opinion piece for CNET's News.com, Rosen made a strong effort to adopt some of the vision of the online industry, in a convincing show that at least she personally did not want to turn back the clock.

"Is the Internet rendering the traditional record business obsolete?" she asked rhetorically, and, no surprise, her answer was "yes." At least the surprise didn't register until you thought about who was writing the essay. This wasn't the typical Internet news commentator, but it could well have been, given the eschatological theme and heavy use of metaphor. "The revolutionary force of the Internet is like a monumental wave, scattering the beach with thousands of new opportunities for delivering content to consumers. Music is a large part of this wave of change, if not the leading ripple in the waters."

Rosen compared music on the Internet to a yard sale with cheap or free goods. It was a giant food court at the mall, with nearly indistinguishable morsels. What record companies offered was like a night out at a swank restaurant. They weren't technophobes at all, but connoisseurs. "When an artist and a record company work together to package an album or song and deliver a unique artistic vision, or when a retailer creates an in-store or home page display of little-known blues singers recommended by a major hip-hop star, this is not a matter of big business skimming profits or homogenizing public taste." Of course, big business skimming profits wouldn't be a matter of delivering unique vision either. In a lawyerly confusion of issues, Rosen didn't say what one had to do with another, but made the point that "marketing and promotion . . . adds value and vigor to the creative community." At least she proved that the RIAA was willing to serve up an opinion piece in the food court of online news. In that brief period it seemed as if a cease-fire agreement was in the works; the industry and the Internet could learn to work together.

The harmony was predictably short-lived: when Napster came along, the talk of piracy, as well as the focus on lawsuits, kicked fast back into high gear.

6

A STAR IS BORN

Brockton, Massachusetts, a small city some twenty miles south of Boston, was a pioneer in the adoption of the urban power grid when its electrical station—the third in the nation—opened in 1883 under the guidance of Thomas Edison himself. By 1884, Brockton would lead the country and the world when its power lines were tapped to charge the electric lights in its city theater, streetlights, streetcars, and fire station. Although Brockton's fortunes as a shoe-making center rose with the Civil War, and sunk by the end of World War II, boxing giant Rocky Marciano would lend pride as the most famous native son until his death in 1969. In 1980, the city would be the birthplace of someone who would later be hailed by some as the first youth hero of the twenty-first century: Shawn Fanning.

Shawn's mother, Colleen, came from a rather poor family of eight children. Despite the tight quarters of the three-bedroom house where the whole family lived, Colleen's older brother threw a house party to fete his graduation and hired a live band for entertainment. If the quarters were cramped for living, that night it was full to bursting with partygoers. The entertainers, with the melodramatic name Macbeth, proved to be a great draw, and a whopping 3,000 people reportedly turned up. While Colleen's younger brother John had the bright idea to hit up the partygoers for some cash, Colleen was distracted by Macbeth's guitarist. The attraction was mutual, and she ended up hitting it off with the charismatic young man, who was actually the scion of what *Business Week* reporter Spencer Ante called "one of the richest families in Massachusetts." The brief encounter left Colleen pregnant. The consequence of music's ability to charm; a meeting of wealth and poverty; conception during an unexpectedly large party from which his uncle hoped to profit, such were the circumstances of Shawn Fanning's beginning. If his life were a novel, the writer would be told to tone down the foreshadowing.

This would be no fairy tale, rags-to-riches meeting. The wealthy guitarist father appeared to have nothing further to do with Colleen or her child, and he left her to raise Shawn by herself. She eventually married another man, an ex-Marine who drove a delivery truck for a living and who moved the new family to Cape Cod, where the couple later had four more children. Despite the fecundity, family life was rocky, and money problems were sometimes overbearing, so Colleen took a job as a nurse's aide. Still they lost their home, the family was split up, and Shawn was forced to live in a foster home for six months. As an outlet, Shawn spent the majority of his free time immersed in playing sports, chiefly basketball and baseball, at which he excelled. Because of his thick, curly tousled hair, Shawn was teasingly nicknamed "Napster."

Though his childhood was sometimes troubled, Fanning had a guardian angel in his uncle John, who'd exploited the rise of computing to lift his own economic fortune with his company, NetGames. Despite a natural reticence that sometimes crossed the line into laziness, with John's encouragement, young Fanning managed to pull himself along to make it into a good college, Northeastern University. He proved to be a bright, if not very diligent, student, given to video gaming and chatting with friends whom he'd made on the Internet. His online tool of choice became Internet Relay Chat, or IRC, a kind of twenty-four-hour free-for-all that had become a de facto meeting place for hackers, traders of copied software and music, and a global

network of more banal conversationalists. Fanning's uncle John provided the computer, and as Shawn's programming skills blossomed, a
part-time job. The rewards were very good, and after a time Fanning,
low-key and usually reticent, was given the keys to his own BMW, a
luxurious car for a college kid and a source of some embarrassment.

It was easy for Fanning to see, on the IRC boards as well as among
the roommates in his dorm, that people were eager to trade music files
on the Internet, but finding good music proved to be the headache. As
he himself grew more immersed, he became convinced that this was a
problem he could solve. Why not him? Fanning saw a gaping opportunity and soon roped in two friends he'd met online, Jordan Ritter, a
twenty-three-year-old fellow Bostonian, and Sean Parker, a twenty-
year-old from Virginia. The trio began to tackle the puzzle of connecting online music traders. Together they would write a program that
would revolutionize computing—they couldn't have realized it would
put them on a collision course with a billion-dollar industry.

Shawn's project was in full production by the beginning of 1999,
and he was pursuing it with all of his being. He had left school without telling any of his teachers and was reportedly writing code around
the clock, in full hacker mode, with little sustenance and even less
sleep. Uncle John couldn't have been more supportive.

While MP3.com was moving ahead full-throttle with IPO money
and Michael Robertson's quest to change the music industry, the Napster trio didn't seem to care at all about the music industry, making
friends, or playing by established rules. All Fanning really wanted was
to make it easier to find music to trade online. The resulting program,
christened "Napster," worked by turning every user's computer into a
small file server, linking all participants together in a giant "you show
me yours, I'll show you mine," dishing up digitized music. In the default setting, the program scanned each user's hard drive to identify all
MP3 files. After sending the names of those files to the central Napster server, anyone searching for a particular song or band would be
able to connect with other users offering such songs for download.

Because Napster itself hosted no music, it allowed the company to
take a hands-off approach, absolving itself from any copyright violations—or so Fanning believed. The program, launched in June 1999,

propagated with unprecedented speed. College students across the country took to Napster like fish to water and were soon assembling libraries of all the songs they could think of. In a matter of months, millions of users began to rely on the program as a kind of ideal swap meet in which all items were free. Since most users' MP3 libraries were made up of copyrighted songs, and Napster users shared mostly commercial music, if users wanted the Rolling Stones's "Satisfaction" or Ol' Dirty Bastard's "I Got Your Money," they could fire up the program and were guaranteed a download in a matter of minutes—so fast it was scary.

Was this further proof of a lawless generation? It would have been easy to draw parallels between the online anarchy and the nature of popular music's influence on society. With the Woodstock twentieth anniversary show that ended in riots, destruction, and several occurrences of rape, this was an argument that neither side wanted to make, even if the popular bands at the center of attention of Napster users, major labels, and Woodstock were often the same. The RIAA couldn't stand idle, however, and on December 7, 1999, the association filed a lawsuit against Napster on behalf of its members. The suit wouldn't reach court for months, though, which gave the program plenty of time to spread.

John Fanning was excited about helping Shawn turn Napster into a business, and he provided the capital for servers and the fat network connections Fanning needed after dropping out of college and losing access to his school's pipes. "I've always thought of him as being my little boy," John told *Business Week*. It was reported that he was hoping to make a movie of Shawn's life.

What effect Napster was having on the record industry's bottom line was hard to tell, but there was no denying that Napster hit Emusic particularly hard—as well as all other Web efforts that hoped users would reach for their wallets when they turned up their speakers. Emusic was forced into giving away portable MP3 players that normally sold for $150 to anyone who bought just twenty-five dollars worth of music. While from Kohn and Hoffman's perspective it was great to see new users becoming familiar with the format that they were selling, competing with free was hard to do. No figures were made public, but selling songs at ninety-nine cents a pop wasn't working. Mjuice, which had similar pricing, sold almost no songs at all.

The success of Napster offered at least intellectual encouragement to some, such as Jim Griffin, who saw it as a validation of his notion that music must "feel free." In the wake of the success of Napster, the most commonly proposed solution became a subscription model, especially favored by industry pundits like Griffin or investors looking for the next wave. "We think that the subscription model is a really interesting one because you can listen to a lot of music, and you don't have to worry about actually transacting on a personal basis, which is very tedious," said Larry Marcus, a partner at Walden VC and former new media analyst with Deutsche Banc Alex Brown. "We are big believers in let people hear the music, and if they hear it, and they like it, then they'll ultimately buy it because the CD is still a great medium."

No one was waiting for the business model to develop, however, and it looked as if the structure of the Internet was quickly altering consumer expectation of what music should cost. Another Internet music phenomenon presaged the MP3 controversy, doing to songbooks what Napster did to songs. Musicians hoping to learn the songs of their favorite bands have usually had two options: buy the published songbooks, which offer the words set to music that rarely fits what their heroes actually play; or listen closely enough to follow along, which is nearly impossible for a beginner. As any eleven-year-old with a new guitar can tell you, other than selling high-priced gear, the industry doesn't do a very good job of helping him out on his way to becoming the next Jimmy Page.

As the Internet grew, fans began to trade their note-for-note transcriptions of songs on the global bulletin board called Usenet in the rec.music.makers.guitar.tablature newsgroup. Soon OLGA, the On Line Guitar Archive, was created on the Web as a way of storing and organizing all of the industrious hands-on research. The community grew and soon over 33,000 songs by hundreds of artists were easily accessible in versions that, if they weren't always perfect, were at least a lot closer than what was available in stores. The transcriptions were also free, which led to increased musical experimentation. A classic rock fan might decide to take a chance and learn a more straight-ahead pop song, just to experiment, which wouldn't happen if he had to pay twenty dollars for a songbook. It wasn't long before the owners of those songs began to complain.

Of course, the metaphors were flying. "There's no difference be-tween someone who posts a guitar tablature online and someone who throws a brick through the front window of Sam the Record Man and steals a CD," said David Basskin, executive director of the Canadian Music Publishers Association. "It's theft."

The National Music Publishers' Association (NMPA) came down hard, as did the publishing wings of labels like EMI, that had been threatening for some time.

In June 1998, OLGA was shut down following legal threats from a rights group, the Harry Fox Agency. Other sites, usually outside of the United States, that ran copy sites, or "mirrors" of the original, continued offering free music. OLGA itself incorporated as a non-profit organization and began a fight for the legality of trading tran-scriptions made by ear, arguing that they are educational tools. From about 33,000 files, OLGA trimmed to about 1,500 purely legal songs, but continued to link to renegade mirrors. A familiar argument about encouragement to buy CDs was made: resparking interest in a partic-ular song would often send a musician to the record store to perfect his playing, which might in turn lead to live, royalty-earning perfor-mances. Those who copied always seemed to fall back on the line that promoting a song's popularity would help its writers, something very hard to prove either way.

Many argued that if the music industry had been more upfront from the beginning and given people decent transcriptions of songs for a more reasonable cost, none of this would have happened. Hal Leonard, a sheet music biggie, responded to online threats by launch-ing Sheet Music Direct. A quick search for a Rolling Stones song found "Beast of Burden" in the online format of choice, tablature, selling for $3.95. But it's hard to compete with free.

As the year 2000 approached, the United States developed a split personality. While the Internet and high tech boosted prosperity and productivity, there was a deep fear that it could be washed away in the blink of an eye. In the countdown to the new millennium, the nation found itself in the grips of a technophobic anxiety as fears of the Y2K bug rose. There was a huge strain on what many had hoped would be the party of a lifetime. Billions of public and private dollars were pumped into modernizing computer networks and the decades-old software that drove public works, emergency response, financial institutions, and airlines. Some heavily bitten paranoiacs bought land far in the country, hoping to ride out an impending fall of civilization that would be triggered by a small oversight in the code underlying some computers. Web sites even sprung up with helpful decorating advice for post-apocalyptic homemakers tired of all the camouflage. By the time the new year finally rolled safely in, there was a palpable sense of relief, if little by way of an apology by those who had fanned the flames of hysteria (or those who had profited wildly from it). The bad memories quickly faded. The new digital bedrock of our civilization had held; if only the bull stock market would stay afloat, the lack of one worldwide party might just be compensated by a long, sustained rise in prosperity.

The fears were understandable, like the fear of flying; something that happens when technology makes leaps that our instincts haven't caught up with yet, and a newly developing world driven by electromagnetic pulses of ones and zeros seemed like magic even to those who understood how things work. The implications of a "global information infrastructure" which, aside from the wire, cable, and servers, exists solely as code, have yet to fully materialize, let alone sink into our human habits and instincts. The realm of myth leaves plenty of space for apocalypse and nightmare, especially when reality begins to function on the level of the fantastic.

Few things could be more fantastic than a network that offered anyone using it a means to communicate and collaborate instantly, shop for homes, stocks, or sandwiches, and publish in real time to a worldwide audience. And nobody would have predicated that once the lines had been laid, a grassroots phenomenon would spring up that seemed capable of turning the Internet into a universal library of music. This would naturally scare and excite those whose music was being added to the library, often without permission. For everyone involved, the possible uses and strange implications of this new system were hard to imagine, as was any resolution that didn't involve massive upset.

Jerky baby steps by the labels—such as releasing only selected promotional songs in safe formats like Liquid or Mjuice—continued to frustrate users. While Mjuice got one track each by Beck and Foo Fighters, whole albums were already on Napster. If the labels were late in sending songs to digitize, anxious employees, such as those who had to write marketing copy on a deadline, could always find the given track on Napster.

If labels and major artists acted like they could barely function online, Napster was clearly master of its domain. Using the program was easier than going to a record store, easier than ordering CDs online, and listeners responded predictably: they ate it up. No one on either side of the skirmish was prepared for this level of success, a rare kind of adoption with every hallmark of a mass movement. The scale and enthusiasm of Napster use trumped all predictions that the online market was exaggerated, or incapable of delivering songs on a gigantic scale. By mid-2000, Napster had around 500,000 people using it every night, a third of the number that typically used AOL at any given time. Songs and artists were rediscovered by listeners whose fond memories wouldn't support a sixteen-dollar CD but who were happy to download a song for a nostalgic listen.

What understandably drove the labels, as well as many artists, crazy was that there was no mechanism in place for them to get paid for this frenzied consumption of music that they either created or held the rights to. This was not to say that no one was profiting. Computer sales were boosted, as later studies would confirm, because Napster demanded faster machines with greater storage capacity. Network infrastructure, from pipeline to consumer, was boosted as well, to respond to consumer demand for high-speed data transfer. As Lars Ulrich would later point out, there were plenty of complaints about how overpriced CDs were from people who seemed to think nothing of shelling out $3,000 for a computer and forty-five dollars a month for DSL service!

Because Napster was spreading with college students as fast as Pokemon with preteens, it was clear that baby steps weren't working, and in 2000, the record industry picked up the pace. Each major label commenced efforts to reach out to consumers online, not just as experiments in community or fan sites, but in actual distribution of their prized catalogs, the music that was the base of each company's profits. Bertelsmann purchased the failing CDNow service, which had tried to be the Amazon.com of CDs, while also joining with Universal to create GetMusic, another online distributor. EMI began talks with Liquid Audio to digitize a chunk of albums. While piece by piece the action looked mostly unexciting, a slow buildup took place, and the momentum was poised to move the industry into a workable position online. There was increasing pressure on label heads from their corporate superiors to resolve a growing crisis, and to do it in a way that made sense for the increasingly wired conglomerates. It was AOL that acquired Time Warner and CNN, not the reverse, and all proposals that ignored online reality were doomed. Bertelsmann also, flush from successful investments in AOL, was itching to move more deeply and boldly online. And Sony, already built on the liberating power of technology, was still hoping to take advantage of the Internet.

But RIAA plans to counter online piracy, chiefly by developing a new set of standards through SDMI, failed to fully bake. Chiariglione, the scientist in charge of developing the standards, was wracked with pressure and responded with a mixture of authoritarianism and despondency. In December 2000, after months of frustrating confusion, he single-handedly dissolved all of SDMI's groups and re-formed them under his leadership. One month later, he simply resigned.

Replacing the CD with another format had long been a pet goal of the labels, and not only because they had made so much money when consumers replaced LPs with CDs and wanted to repeat the process. The CD, as any kid with an interest in MP3s can tell you, is a fundamentally insecure format. There is no copy protection, and no watermarking to trace the music's origin. Anyone can copy any CD as often as he'd like, by making MP3s or tapes, or even burning a hundred duplicate CDs on a home burner. Remember, a CD burner costs less than the price of seven CDs.

BMG, for one, was on the prowl for technical solutions, and seemed willing to strike out on its own, if necessary. In Germany—a country in which Napster wasn't so big, but where burning CDs was the primary focus of music trading—the company attempted to remedy the situation. In January, BMG partnered with the Israeli firm Midbar to release two albums using its Cactus Data Shield technology, which prevented owners of the CDs from copying them with burners. After releasing about 100,000 discs in the new format, however, because of problems with compatibility, the company got so many returns that it canceled the experiment and replaced the returns with nonprotected discs. The companies vowed to renew the effort at a later date. Other plans for a complete revamping of the CD were undertaken by Philips and Sony, as DVD audio appeared on the horizon promising a new physical format with new features that might make the loss of some freedom a little more palatable. Efforts like these were met with resistance from consumer groups and online freedom advocates, who pointed out that the law allowed for owners of CDs to make personal copies. Crafting technical solutions that infringed on consumer rights was an unfortunate route to travel, the critics argued.

But in the United States, it was the MP3 file that was the chief means of widespread music sharing. Despite, or perhaps because of, a devoted and enthusiastic user base that was growing exponentially, Napster was taking hits from all sides, and everyone knew that it wouldn't be long until an artist stepped up to challenge the legality, not to mention morality, of Fanning's brainchild. The shocker was the group that did the challenging.

Metallica, a San Francisco–based heavy metal band that had since the '80s sustained a career that had been launched by tape swapping, and that encouraged fans to tape their shows and trade them, seemed an unlikely candidate for outrage over unauthorized trading.

The group had forged a strong base of fans by keeping it real and ignoring the hairspray, spandex, and makeup look popular when they started. While sticking to what they did best, rocking hard and treating fans like grownups, the group had found itself on the top of the heap, nearly the lone group among contemporaries to survive over a twenty-year period. The band had always carefully asserted its rights when it could, for instance insisting on owning the master recordings of its songs, a rare luxury since bands are usually pressured by labels to give up these lucrative chips. But Metallica members were far from control freaks when it came to live recordings and stuck with a taping policy that was generally in line with the Grateful Dead. The band even included a section in their official fanzine in which readers could rate various CD, tape, and vinyl bootlegs.

At the end of the 1990s, however, the band had found itself in uncharted waters. Members had cut their locks and submitted to makeovers that updated their stoner, Beavis-and-Butthead images. They had also begun recording music for a movie soundtrack, in particular a song titled "I Disappear." Work on the song was progressing slowly, and the band, feeling uncomfortable, had still not settled on a releasable version. In the midst of this vulnerable moment came word that not one but at least three versions they'd been working on had not only slipped out, but were being freely traded by fans online, particularly users of Napster. They looked into it and found out that all of their songs were being traded. For Metallica, this crossed a line. Like the Grateful Dead, they had always made a distinction between music recorded at a concert and music that they had slaved for months over in a studio. On April 13, 2000, the band's attorney, Howard King, filed suit against University of Southern California, Indiana University, Yale University, and Napster, alleging that Napster, and the universities that allowed its use, violated the Racketeering Influenced and Corrupt Organizations Act, a piece of legislation that had originally been aimed at organized crime.

The suit was ironic because Indiana University had once banned Napster, claiming it was a bandwidth hog. The school paper ran an editorial in agreement, under the headline "Good Riddance to

Napster.com." The piece argued, "Students attempting to hunker down to coursework should not have to be inconvenienced by a strain on the network." But students at IU, like students at Northwestern and Oregon State, had fought back against Napster bans, often using '60s-style activist jargon. In February 2000, one IU student, Chad Paulson, organized a petition drive to keep universities from banning the program, decrying what he claimed was "censorship." The university rescinded its ban. For IU to then be named in a lawsuit was a bitter pill. Napster was soon forbidden on campus for a second time. Eventually over 200 colleges and universities banned use of the program over their networks. Others, like MIT, Stanford, and Princeton, refused to cave, under grounds of free speech. "MIT has had a long history of providing its faculty, staff, and students with uncensored access to the Internet and its vast array of resources," said James Bruce, vice president of MIT, in a note to Metallica's lawyer. "This policy is consistent with MIT's educational mission and our deeply held values of academic freedom."

For students who found themselves at the schools that banned Napster, David Weekly responded by posting information on his site that would help set up workarounds. This was the second time that Weekly publicly assisted Napster users (as opposed to the company, which he seemed to view simply as a means to an end). His first effort was posting the results of a four-hour analysis he did of Napster protocols, tracking the way the servers communicated with users' programs. The company reacted by asking Weekly to remove his page, which he "politely refused" to do, pointing out the irony to a CNET reporter. "Fundamentally I think that it's not something that's harmful to Napster," said Weekly. "But more than that, it's in line with the ideals Napster embodies: the discovery and sharing of information. The irony is not lost on me that their sole business is distributing the information of other people."

While filing suits against universities for allowing their students to use school networks to download copyrighted works, Metallica's lawyer Howard King also asked Napster to remove any Metallica songs from its servers. Napster responded by claiming that this was an impossible request, given that files were named by users, making their elimination impossible. Besides, once a service provider started taking control of content, it risked further suits. Instead, Napster's lawyers invited King to provide names of anyone found trading copyrighted songs, offering to expel them. King, and the band, rose to the challenge.

Napster users who were bumped from the system as a result of Metallica's suit didn't take kindly to the action, and 30,000 of them petitioned the company to let them back on. Napster invoked the terms of the Digital Millennium Copyright Act to let protesting users off the hook, a sign that the company's legal sophistication was rising. Under the terms of the DMCA, Metallica had ten days to take legal action against identified users who disputed their guilt; otherwise they would be allowed back on the service. For a band, and for an industry, that was taking pains to be seen as fighting the service, not the fan, prosecution was clearly a route to avoid. That didn't stop King from complaining bitterly about the protesters' veracity. "They're perjuring themselves. They're not misidentified. We did a survey and we have proof that at such-and-such a date, they were offering Metallica songs. Could there be ten mistakes? Sure. Fifteen? Maybe. But there are not 17,000 mistakes. There's no way."

Fanning reacted, in press releases, by bemoaning the lack of record companies and artists working with Napster. His sincerity on this point was questionable, however, as those who had talked with him informally would attest. "Shawn has no issues with copyright," said Rob Lord, who by then had become Fanning's friend and fellow–Bay area resident. "He just has no issues!"

Reactions to Metallica's aggressive stand ranged widely, from diehard support to anger and accusations of betrayal. In a story in Salon, Brian Lew called Metallica's fight "stunningly ironic in light of the band's history," which was that "before Metallica even recorded their debut album, the band had established a worldwide following via an underground tape-trading network." That, Lew argued, was the same type of network that was now being dismissed as "illegal and unrestricted copying and distribution."

The most satirical reactions took center stage. A Web site called PayLars.com opened to collect donations from fans who were feeling guilty and wanted to give something back to Metallica. Sites like MetallicaSucks.com and BoycottMetallica.com made their intentions plain. NewGrounds.com made a funny downloadable animation about "the definitive sell-out band Metallica." An even more popular animation made by Camp Chaos, "Napster Bad," made its way around the world virally, by e-mail from viewer to viewer. It featured a beastlike interpretation of guitarist James Hetfield and a particularly smarmy Ulrich. The animation proved so popular that its creators launched a series of follow-ups. The media did much to publicize the excitements and the lawsuits, but it was also particularly tiresome for Metallica. If Fanning was being toasted by everyone from *Wired* to MTV, a brush with fame was nothing new for Ulrich, and a new American tour kept him distracted.

Another of King's clients, LA rap superstar Dr. Dre, was roped into the drama. In May, soon after the Metallica copyright infringement lawsuit, King filed another suit on Dre's behalf. He too delivered a list of names, nearly as large as Metallica's. Eminem, Dre's young white protégé and newly arrived king of the charts, was quick to join the media circus. Weeks before his new CD, *The Marshall Mathers LP*, was due to hit stores, songs from the CD were being traded with abandon on Napster. Eminem was infuriated and vented his spleen to reporters.

"Whoever put my s—t on the Internet, I want to meet that motherf—ker and beat the s—t out of him," Eminem was quoted as saying in *Wall of Sound*, "because I picture this scrawny little dickhead going, 'I got Eminem's new CD! I got Eminem's new CD! I'm going to put it on the Internet.' I think that anybody who tries to make excuses for that s—t is a f—king bitch. I'm sorry; when I worked 9 to 5, I expected to get a f—king paycheck every week. It's the same with music; if I'm putting my f—king heart and all my time into music, I expect to get rewarded for that. I work hard . . . and anybody can just throw a computer up and download my s—t for free." He challenged the validity of claims that young people couldn't afford to pay for music by saying that before he was successful he could never afford a computer, but made sure to pay for music by his favorite bands. "If you can afford a computer, you can afford to pay $16 for my CD." Slashing men and raping women, fine. Violence against gays, sure. Copying a CD? That shit's wack!

There was a question over how much Metallica, Dre, and Eminem understood exactly what they were fighting. While his depth of knowledge obviously increased as the weeks rolled by, at the time of the confrontation at the Napster offices, Ulrich admitted that he didn't use the Internet and even had trouble getting online with the easiest service around, AOL. Rapper Ice-T reasoned that the bands were being manipulated by their lawyer, King. "I don't even think Dr. Dre and all them know why they're mad," he said. "I think their lawyer called them up. If my lawyer called me up and said I can make you a couple million dollars, I'd be like, 'do it.'" Ulrich, of course, saw things differently, and as part of his campaign to raise awareness of his point of view, he agreed to be interviewed by the readers of Slashdot.org, a Web site of news and commentary run by and for "nerds"—most of whom were devoted to the open-source software movement, champions of the Linux operating system, a crowd known to be very skeptical of any effort to hinder their online freedom.

"Are we assholes for wanting to get off this service that I was never asked if I wanted to be part of in the first place?" Ulrich asked. He seemed to take particular offense to claims that Metallica was only fighting Napster because the band was being greedy. "There's one thing that people kind of keep forgetting, which is that Napster, they have this sort of innocent smirk in front of their face and they hold up their hand and they go 'We're not really pirates, we're not really doing anything illegal, we're just offering a service,' but what people have to remember, and obviously some of this has developed in the last month, is that Napster is a corporation, OK? They just got $15 million in funding from some of the major venture capitalists out here. They have all along, ultimately getting to the point where they could have a major IPO, which is the one option, or get basically bought out by an AOL type of company. So at some point there will be a major, major profit going on for the people who've invested in Napster. And that money is basically the same as profiting from stolen property."

Despite the animosity, record executives couldn't help but be impressed by Napster from every angle including the ease of use and the system's incredible popularity. Ted Cohen was representative in this regard, though with a bit more hands-on experience. He admitted to using Napster to find songs that he owned but couldn't bother to track down. "Personal opinion," he offered in June, "Napster is a pretty cool thing. I ran into Napster a year ago May, I started talking to them in June, they offered me the CEO position in October, I started working with them in November." While he didn't accept the CEO offer, Cohen became a consultant, to both Napster and the major labels.

"I think it's one of the coolest things to come around. I also thought the moment I saw it 'My God! This could destroy the whole business.' If I steal from you and it's clever and it's cool, it's OK? If I break down your door with a sledgehammer, that's not cool, but if I figure out a way to rip you off electronically, then everything's all right? I find myself being seduced by the same thing, going 'it's so bad, but it's so cool.' How do you take something like this and turn it into something that the industry really could use?"

Around the same time, Bertelsmann CEO Thomas Middelhoff said something similar to an audience at the PopKomm conference in Cologne, Germany, a forward-looking statement that made some noises towards a resolution with at least the idea of Napster.

"Let's be honest. Despite all the dangers, Napster is pretty cool," he said, adding that the system had "an excellent music brand transporting the following characteristics: High quality, free delivery of music directly into your home, simple use, global selection from the repertory of all labels, prompt service and uncoupled program selection."

Middelhoff called "file-sharing as a system . . . a great idea," but he said Fanning's mistake was "not having developed a complementary system for the protection of intellectual property rights and combining the two."

He went on to criticize the reaction of the record industry to the Internet, saying it was too slow and didn't anticipate the speed of the development on the Net. He even described the labels' reactions to Napster as "defensive posturing and distancing," and ended by calling for a balance between legal tactics and technical development. If Middlehoff's subordinates, the label bosses at BMG, were listening, his comments must have come as a sharp rebuke, or a premonition of things to come.

Other entertainment lawyers didn't see things on the same terms that Howard King did. Speaking directly to the success of the hitmakers that topped the year's charts, Ken Hertz espoused the theory that Napster was actually helping propel their success, possibly with the complicity of the marketing departments at their respective labels. "'N Sync, Britney Spears, and Eminem were the three most heavily trafficked artists at Napster the week before their records came out, and those records were the fastest selling records of all time," Hertz said. "Whether you like it or not, it is a huge promotional tool," which could be used in that regard, "without people standing on ceremony and saying they philosophically oppose Napster. That's just bullshit. My guess is that the marketing guys at Jive, and at Interscope, seeded Napster with new releases, with pre-release copies of that music, because the minute those songs hit the radio they're going to be on Napster anyway."

The success wasn't necessarily limited to those who would stay at a label, Hertz theorized. "I think that kids trading files on the Internet is one of the greatest things that ever happened to musicians that were otherwise caught in a ridiculous marketing stranglehold by the consolidation of the radio industry, and the consolidation in the record industry."

The consolidation, he said, "created this problem" which was that retailers were having trouble making money, record companies were having trouble marketing records through radio and other channels, "and so as a result it's extraordinarily difficult to break records," because the costs to penetrate the cartel were so high. "What happens is that kids have a tough time discovering new music. I mean that clearly: kids will tell you all the time that they're dying to discover new music, but the problem is the ways that they discover new music,

even if it's old music that they've never heard before, are typically radio and word of mouth, that's it. And so on some level file sharing online is radio and word of mouth. I would argue that Napster seems to
behave a lot more like interactive radio than it does as a surrogate for
retail." That was a powerful voice of support that would be echoed by
the actions of artists that Hertz represented, like Courtney Love.

But Hertz was hedging his bets. At the same time he had investments
in both MusicMarc, an Israeli company working on a file-protection
system, and was working with those developing Uprizer, a service that
embraced a future in which copyright was no longer enforceable.

While Hilary Rosen had been hoping to change the public's per-
ception that the RIAA was the cruelly litigious defender of an unfair
status quo, Napster's massive popularity could not go unanswered.
On June 12, 2000, the association filed for a preliminary injunction, a
court order that would shut down the service before the pending trial,
citing widespread copyright infringement that would cause the industry great harm. Along with the expected legal and industry folks, the
RIAA motion was accompanied by a supportive declaration from
Michael Robertson, a surprise that was trumpeted at the head of the
RIAA's press release. Robertson, in the midst of his own industry lawsuit, was hoping that the contrast with Napster might help his own
case and was presenting MP3.com as the anti-Napster, a move that
was widely regarded as "selling out" by file-trading supporters.

"I signed the declaration against Napster because I fundamentally
think it's not sound," Robertson said in his defense, and it was hard to
doubt his sincerity, especially when it came to his commitment to the
marketplace and its protections. As someone who spent his time inventing new schemes to package and sell music, he wanted those protections there for him, later. Besides, he had spent the last half year trying hard to position himself as the blonde angel to the Napster devil.

While trading and downloading songs had become the rage,
Robertson was itching to prove that the stock market had been correct
in regarding MP3.com so highly. But how could he top Napster,
which seemed to offer access to nearly every musical piece a person
could want? He decided to play an entirely different game: he would

offer a product that would give users what they already had! The idea was sound: let anyone who owns a CD have access to that music over the Web, no matter where the original disc was. Other companies were offering something similar that let users copy their CDs and upload them to a private locker that they could access anywhere. While nice when all that music was finally in one's locker, getting it there was an enormous chore. Robertson's Beam-It would be different by verifying that users actually had a CD in their computers, and then, instead of ripping and uploading all the songs, it would just note in the records that the particular user owned the album. To stream back the album, Beam-It would pull from a vast database, a digital library ripped from over 40,000 discs that the company had bought. Robertson's vision was of a service that enabled the consumers to "space shift" their CD collections; it didn't actually matter whether what was being streamed came from the consumer's CD or the MP3.com's, as long as the recording was the same. The service was launched January 12, 2000.

The model was compelling. It was easy to imagine getting around the rules by borrowing a friend's CDs to fool Beam-It into thinking you owned them, but if consumers were going to go to that trouble, they might just as well make copies. In spirit, Beam-It was much closer to the traditional sense of ownership. But in practice, the RIAA sued. The thrust of the suit, which was filed on behalf of the big five labels January 21 in federal court in New York, was that MP3.com didn't have the right to build its business on the backs of labels, and since the labels hadn't given Robertson permission to stream his company's copies of CDs, it didn't matter if the consumer owned a particular CD or not. "Simply put, it is not legal to compile a vast database of our members' sound recordings with no permission and no license," said Hilary Rosen in a letter to Robertson posted on MP3.com. "Obviously, you are not free to take protected works simply because you want them." There were precedents that established that you could make a duplicate of a copyrighted work for your own use, but it wasn't legal for a company to do that for you.

The RIAA asked for a summary judgment to shut down the service, and on April 28 Judge Jed Rakoff of the southern district court of

New York complied and issued an order for Robertson to remove the offending files, which essentially shut Beam-It down. Because of a possible fine of $150,000 per song, when the company had digitized as many as 40,000 CDs, the damages could easily bankrupt the company. Robertson began negotiating like crazy with any label that would strike a deal, but by April MP3.com stock was down to six and a half dollars a share. Late that month, there seemed to be a thaw in the relationship between Robertson and Rosen, who said in an interview with *Salon's* Janelle Brown that "The business models that MP3.com have put forward are interesting business models. The issue with MP3.com is simply of them not seeking licenses prior to the launching of their system."

Robertson remained hurt and felt deeply misunderstood. "Most people don't understand what happened," he said. "It's just painted so simply as a copyright violation and they just assume it's like Napster." But Beam-It was "really the opposite of Napster. It says that you don't get any music until you've paid for it, but once you've paid for it, you should get access to it digitally if that's the way you want to listen to it." He was frustrated because his message of computer age reform had been "drowned out" by Napster, and because the suit against his company was aiding the RIAA's real enemy. "If you don't give people who buy the music the right to listen to it, you remove the incentive to buy the music!" Ever the outsider hoping bring people together—with a cut for himself if possible—Robertson's praise of Napster echoed Middelhoff's. "Napster's great for the consumer, no doubt about it. What's missing from Napster is that balance. It also has to be beneficial for the copyright owner, that's what's missing from Napster. The courts are still wrestling with whether it's illegal or not, and I don't know about that, but in my mind Napster violates the spirit of the copyright law. The spirit says there's got to be a balance, there's got to be a win for consumers and a win for the people who make the music so they'll continue to make music."

Meanwhile, a feeding frenzy was developing as soon as MP3.com blood was smelled. The biggest suit was filed by the Harry Fox Agency on behalf of two of its major clients, MPL Communication and Peer International. Because MPL was partly owned by Paul

McCartney, Robertson sent him an open letter, explaining the service "as a businessman and not a lawyer." The letter began, "I don't know if you're aware or not, but a publishing company you own a portion of filed a lawsuit against my company last week. I wanted to drop you a note explaining what we're doing because my suspicion is that you're not involved in these types of decisions and may not know exactly what is happening. I think after an explanation, perhaps you'll change your mind." The letter ended with a final plea, and as ever, an offer to run a demo. "We worked hard to build a responsible system. We'd love to have you down to our office for a personal demo and to discuss the situation, anytime." In May, large independent TVT Records filed a similar suit.

On May 4, Judge Rakoff delivered his opinion, which began by stating how cut and dried he felt the Beam-It case was. "The complex marvels of cyberspatial communication may create difficult legal issues; but not in this case," he wrote, expressing that he felt that MP3.com's infringements of copyright were "clear." "Although defendant seeks to portray its service as the 'functional equivalent' of storing its subscribers' CDs, in actuality defendant is re-playing for the subscribers converted versions of the recordings it copied, without authorization, from plaintiffs' copyrighted CDs." Further diminishing MP3.com's arguments that the service helped labels sell more records, Rakoff wrote "Such arguments—though dressed in the garb of an expert's 'opinion' (that, on inspection, consists almost entirely of speculative and conclusory statements)—are unpersuasive. Any allegedly positive impact of defendant's activities on plaintiffs' prior market in no way frees defendant to usurp a further market that directly derives from reproduction of the plaintiffs' copyrighted works." Even if a new market hasn't been fully developed by the owners of copyright, "a copyright holder's 'exclusive' rights, derived from the Constitution and the Copyright Act, include the right, within broad limits, to curb the development of such a derivative market by refusing to license a copyrighted work or by doing so only on terms the copyright owner finds acceptable." Copyright, the judge wrote, was not about providing "consumer convenience," but protecting a copyright holder's property interests. The only thing Rakoff didn't deliver was the final tally of damages for which MP3.com would be held liable. Robertson and his team began to negotiate a settlement with the labels in earnest and with wallets out.

Rapper and actor Ice-T, a longtime supporter of MP3.com, believed that the labels were acting like gangsters. "The labels know that they're not valuable; nobody gives a fuck about Sony; they care about the artist," he explained. With the rise of the Internet and its individual empowerment, "The record label is cut out if it doesn't figure a way to get into the loop. And the way they do it is they sue motherfuckers right now, and try to break them down. That's gangster tactics. Gangsters work like that."

More dispiriting was speculation that whatever the award, especially with a negotiated settlement, the artists whose works were being licensed would probably not get anything, because the license would be classified as a "blanket licensing" agreement. Whitney Broussard, a New York entertainment lawyer with a background working for labels as well as directly for artists, explained: "Ironically record contracts generally say that the artist specifically does not participate in income generated from blanket licenses. This provision is *not* in there accidentally or an artifact of bygone days, it is in there *specifically* to make sure that the artist never saw a dime of the public performance income generated from sound recordings outside the U.S."

"These are, of course," Broussard pointed out, "the very same record companies who love to discuss how artists are getting ripped off by consumers. They obviously appreciate the fact that your average Joe could care less about the economic impact of his actions on the world's largest media companies."

The bad news in the courts dampened investor enthusiasm for the online music companies. While the Net sector in general had slowed dramatically, for online music companies things were even worse. Firms like Emusic and Mjuice were not selling enough music, at ninety-nine cents or a dollar a song, to justify their expenses, and it didn't seem they would anytime soon.

In March, Artist Direct had peered confidently into a IPO-driven future of success. Like going down a list, Geiger's company had picked up other online properties such as Mjuice, which navigated ground that fell somewhere between Liquid Audio and Emusic, offering songs for sale and for free to promote its protection format. Investment and artists' deals with Artist Direct were likewise very high, as everyone wanted a stake in the company that seemed destined to bring Silicon Valley–style instant riches to Hollywood. Four of the five big labels, Sony, BMG, Warner, and Universal, ponied up a total of $97.5 million in the company's third round of financing. The company hoped to raise $86 million more through an IPO. Options had been distributed far and wide within the artist community also, encouraged by Artist Direct's aim of facilitating one-on-one relationships between artists and audiences. Beck, Beastie Boys, Tom Petty, and Cher were among those with a stake in the offering, and some volunteered to appear in a video made for the company's "road show" to persuade investors, a rather embarrassing effort that showed Cher and Petty appearing about as authoritative as George W. Bush in a foreign policy quiz.

Unfortunately, after a short sputtering start in which shares priced at twelve dollars, raising $60 million, they soon fell far below that, and never recovered. To make matters worse, the company violated SEC regulations by issuing too many options, and a buyback program threatened to cost the company $24 million—nearly half its IPO gain. The mood was predictably glum, even while most analysts continued to point to the company as one that was leading the way. Still, for a company that told its new workers that they could expect to encounter "Marilyn Manson walking down the hall" or to attend a company picnic at which Prince might perform, the glamour was starting to wear off.

* * *

While MP3.com was taking its blows, Napster was being employed for more purposes all the time. In April, a program called Wrapster was released that let its users bundle any type of files in a "wrapper" that made Napster identify it as a single MP3. Thus movies, pornography, and pirated software could be distributed taking advantage of Napster's popularity and reliability. Shady uses aside, the ability to trade files using peer-to-peer, or P2P as it was becoming known, was an idea that took the Net world by storm, especially at the top, among companies and developers whose business it was to predict where things were going and get to work on them before anyone else. P2P, as a writer for tech publisher O'Reilly explained, "makes the Internet interesting again." Impressed by the power unleashed by the decentralized model of computing, tech companies as staid as Microsoft were embracing many of its principles, at least as a buzzword to throw around at conferences.

With all guns aimed at it, Napster was desperately in need of a hero. Or failing that, a strong injection of cash. If Napster was a truly inspired piece of software, it was also true that the company it spawned was not run very well. From Uncle John's often misguided scheming and prognostications, to executive Eileen Richardson's reportedly abrasive personality, the ship was adrift and taking on water.

Hummer Winblad—the same company that financed Liquid Audio's protection scheme—stepped up. In May, Napster closed its first round of funding with the venture firm, for $15 million. Along with the infusion of capital, the investors provided a solid, sensible new CEO, Hank Barry. Along with plenty of high-tech venture background, Barry provided something else that the infant company needed: a strong background in law, with a specialty in intellectual property. At Stanford, where he received a law degree, Barry had won a national prize for a paper on copyright. He promised to not only build a working business model for the company, but also to help it solve its legal problems. He was well-versed on the history of Internet technology and the goals of its creators. He told *Salon* interviewer Damien Cave that the Internet was "originally formed so that academics could share files. The Internet is a file-sharing application. So it's great to be involved with something that's so Net-basic." In July, the former Universal vice president of digital music, Keith Bernstein, was hired, as his former company pushed harder than anyone against Napster.

While Lars Ulrich, Dr. Dre, Eminem, and Busta Rhymes had assumed the mantle of embattled musicians fighting for their rights against the hordes unleashed by Napster's unholy application, they were soon joined by others, such as Noah Stone's Artists Against Piracy coalition, a group that stuck pretty closely to the big-label line, and, no surprise, received funding from the RIAA and Walt Disney. Others had been lined up on the pro-Napster side, such as Chuck D and Limp Bizkit (after a $2 million tour sponsorship). Most artists remained much more ambivalent to both sides, knowing first hand that record companies were not looking out for their benefit. Ice-T was among this camp and found it hard to talk about the issue without raising contradictions.

"Copyright is important to certain people. Most of the cats that are [talking about it being outdated] have never created anything," he said. "There's a point where you cross the line and you are robbing people. You've got to realize that there are a lot of people who are counting on this stuff for their life savings, and this is their money, and it is important. It's very touchy. Just put it all out there for free? Food should be free then, right? Food and water should be free, and nobody should have to pay to live and eat or nothing, you know? If you create something you're entitled to some kind of money or reward or something if somebody else wants it, ain't nothing wrong with that. But when your record is on the radio it's free. It's really hard to break it down the middle."

Courtney Love was another artist who harbored mixed feelings. What she'd experienced in the industry, though, was enough for her to want to speak out about it. Straight from a speech a few days earlier at the Million Mom March about the need gun for control, a subject she supported from the painful experience of losing her husband, Kurt Cobain, to a gun-inflicted suicide, Love was fired up with righteous anger.

Backstage at the Digital Hollywood Conference in New York on May 16, Love rehearsed her notes with her lawyer and adviser, Ken Hertz. While her crew had searched for the past few weeks for someone to write Love's keynote, they had returned empty-handed, and it had fallen on Hertz to draft much of what she said, a task he approached with gusto. While Love was upset by the paparazzi that had appeared in the audience, she took the stage grinning and moving with the punk rock swagger that had gotten her where she was.

"Today I want to talk about piracy and music," she announced, playing up the concern of the moment. "What is piracy? Piracy is the act of stealing an artist's work without any intention of paying for it. I'm not talking about Napster-type software. I'm talking about major label recording contracts."

She then led the crowd through the money involved in a hypothetical band's first year after signing with a major label. The equation was a familiar one to those who knew Hertz, who often used it to illustrate just how badly artists were typically treated by big label contracts. After a million-dollar advance and a million record sales, which put the hypothetical band at the level of success higher than the vast majority, the group is left with nothing but a year of exciting memories, not even owning the work that they sweated long and hard for. The record company? "Their profit is $6.6 million; the band may as well be working at a 7-Eleven," Love explained.

Love recited a litany of grievances with the RIAA, such as the work-for-hire amendment, which, while it was supposed to grant artists the rights to their domain name, also slipped in a provision that let record companies own the domain if an artist creates a work for hire for them. "Although I've never met anyone at a record company who 'believed in the Internet,' they've all been trying to cover their asses by securing everyone's digital rights. Not that they know what to do with them. Go to a major label–owned band site. Give me a dollar for every time you see an annoying 'under construction' sign. I used to pester Geffen (when it was a label) to do a better job. I was totally ignored for two years, until I got my band name back. The Goo Goo Dolls are struggling to gain control of their domain name from Warner Bros., who claim they own the name because they set up a shitty promotional Web site for the band." That, she said, was piracy.

"Story after story gets told about artists—some of them in their 60s and 70s, some of them authors of huge successful songs that we all enjoy, use, and sing—living in total poverty, never having been paid anything. Not even having access to a union or to basic health care. Artists who have generated billions of dollars for an industry die broke and uncared-for. And they're not actors or participators.

They're the rightful owners, originators, and performers of original compositions. This is piracy. Technology is not piracy."

But Love also asserted her support for Ulrich, though she criticized him for not being able to get his message across in a succinct sound bite. "How dare they behave in such a horrified manner in regards to copyright law when their entire industry is based on piracy? When Mister Label Head Guy, whom my lawyer yelled at me not to name, got caught last year selling millions of 'cleans' out the back door. 'Cleans' being the records that aren't for marketing but are to be sold. Who the fuck is this guy? He wants to save a little cash so he fucks the artist and goes home? Do they fire him? Does Chuck Phillips of the *LA Times* say anything? No way! This guy's a source! He throws awesome dinner parties! Why fuck with the status quo? Let's pick on Lars Ulrich instead because he brought up an interesting point!"

The speech was lengthy, rambling, sometimes adolescent, and internally inconsistent, but it was by most standards a brave and worthy effort that got the word far out, reaching audiences that probably never paid attention to Love before. Salon.com reprinted the text in its entirety, and it became one of the most viewed pages the site had ever published. There was some criticism by those who believed that Courtney's walk through of the band's recording contract was stolen from a piece written by Chicago punk legend, Big Black's Steve Albini. Albini's piece was published in underground journal *The Baffler* years earlier. This was false, unless Hertz himself had been riffing on Albini's piece for years. Either way, Hertz certainly had enough experience negotiating deals to know the figures himself.

*   *   *

In the end, Love's call to arms was this: every band had nothing to lose and everything to gain from using the Internet to develop a deeply personal relationship with their fans, a relationship that record labels, or "distributors" as she preferred to call them, simply couldn't understand. She was not afraid of MP3s, she said, but was happy to let anyone sample her work and decide if it was something that they wanted to have as part of their lives. Music was, after all, a "service," and all artists worked for tips, she explained. She was willing to toss aside all the accouterments of fame and celebrity if it meant a more meaningful relationship with her fans. Noble sentiments that rose above the more cynical swipes at her efforts. Only her actions could prove whether or not she meant what she said.

Emboldened by Dre, Chuck D, Eminem, and Love, other artists started jumping into the fray, ready to fight for their rights. Continuing the dialogue, but with stronger gangster affect, Busta Rhymes joined in. "I think the whole Napster thing is horrible. I think that it's probably one of the worst things that was ever invented, and at the end of the day, if they touch my music, it's going to get dealt with accordingly," said Rhymes in an MTV interview. "I'm pretty sure they don't really give a f—k. But for those that don't care, there are consequences. If they continue to do what they do, knowing how disappointed the artists are—credible, top-of-the-line dons in the game that have an issue with it—and if they're going to disregard all of that, then justice is a reward. They will be dealt with accordingly."

The top-of-the-line dons were trying to imagine their response and were betting on the courts and the lawmakers. But the amount of interest that Napster had generated left them no other choice but to move forward with online projects of one sort or another. As guru to many in the developing online music space, Jim Griffin had plenty of advice to dispense. One of his main pieces was that if a company wanted to succeed online, it needed to get past the mentality of a truck owner, and do anything it could to make their artists known.

"Their business is based on products and trucks," Griffin said. "I've found that there's a remarkable difference—and I know that these businesses are generally all owned by the same people—there is a remarkable difference between those companies that owned trucks directly, and those that did not. Geffen never owned a truck; Interscope never owned a truck; Maverick never owned a truck. These companies, though they were owned and funded by bigger companies, had the kind of radical sensibilities of those that didn't own a distribution system. Their only motive was to cut through the clutter of the marketplace, and that's a wonderful motivation for this new world, and speaks volumes as to why they were successful and were worth acquiring to these big companies. But the motivation of those big companies was that they owned a lot of trucks, a lot of warehouses, and a lot of CD pressing plants. And furthermore, control over quantity and destiny of product is essential to running a product-based business. If you're in the product business you have to control the quantity and the destiny of the products you distribute, because if you don't then the price falls to the marginal cost of delivery, and that can be pretty savage. And that's what we're seeing now. Napster isn't so much about piracy as it is pricing, because quite simply price falls to at or near marginal cost."

Marginal cost on the Internet, thanks to Shawn Fanning, was about zero.

7

No One to Blame

There has grown up in the minds of certain groups in this country the notion that because a man or a corporation has made a profit [from] the public for a number of years, the government and the courts are charged with the duty of guaranteeing such profit in the future, even in the face of changing circumstances and contrary public interest. This strange doctrine is not supported by statute nor common law. Neither individuals nor corporations have any right to come into court and ask that the clock of history be stopped, or turned back, for their private benefit.

Robert A. Heinlein, "Life-Line"

Whether its principals are menacingly corrupt and repulsively shallow, or solid, upright businesspeople with a deep love and respect for genius in art and honesty in commerce, it is hard to make the case the music industry is anything other than middlemen. And while no one disputes that the agents of promotion and distribution can add much to the appreciation of works of popular art and culture, it seems natural that middlemen should be replaced when something better comes along. Or at least should change with the times. Unless you believe the argument made by jaded music business types that unpackaged music is so pervasive and of so little worth that by funding, packaging, and promoting artists, the labels are the ones doing the actual creative work of value.

Where the Net is fast and commonly accessible, enthusiasts have come to depend on it to get their music. The problems that Internet distribution of music solve are those of convenience and distance. That songs were free (and still are) for a lot of college students and others clever enough to be keyed into a network was an obvious incentive: Who wouldn't want a library of free music? This was enough to spur the initial users to overcome many inconveniences of music on the computer. (That they were already fairly chained to their computers was another factor.) Threatened with the trend against middlemen that the Internet seemed to represent ("disintermediation" was the catchphrase of the year), record labels tried to put on the brakes. But the brakes only seemed to work for the labels' own train, while other cars roared past into online convenience and excitement, and the labels were not there to collect fees.

"The record industry didn't foresee Napster, the record industry didn't think of any of these things, and yet they are scrambling to find ways after the fact to react to them, and then to take advantage of them," said Jim Griffin.

Napster was simply an idea whose time had come, and Fanning perhaps the lucky first person to do the necessary coding. Very soon, a tidal wave of imitators appeared. The potential of college administrators to ban Napster use, as well the looming court cases poised to obliterate the service, were problems addressed by Justin Frankel and Tom Pepper of Nullsoft.

Gnutella, the most famous of the Napster copycats, was released in March by Frankel and the Nullsoft team. It came as a shock to music industry insiders and to hackers alike. When Nullsoft was bought for a princely sum of $100 million by AOL Time Warner, Frankel had been expected to give up his role as media provocateur and enfant terrible, handing over the mantel to newer faces like Fanning. But, sure enough, there on the Nullsoft website on March 13 was the beta version of Gnutella, a tool that seemed poised to take on Napster as the key program for online file sharing.

It got its name from a playful combination of GNU, a leading organization in the open-source software movement, and a creamy Italian chocolate spread.

Despite Nullsoft's position in the very belly of the emerging media beast, its developers unleashed the software in an open-source format. Gnutella worked by turning users, as well as developers, into solo agents who communicated with each other in a distributed network, without a central server to act as a database of available songs, as with Napster. Because the search for songs was written to be "peer-to-peer" or P2P, functioning like a long chain of inquiry from user to user, once released the program would still work even if its creator's company were shut down. Because it was written as open source—its code open for all to see and modify—even if were disowned by its creators, it could continue to be developed.

Although Frankel may have posted his sly creation without much fanfare, it was received with immediate enthusiasm, and word spread around the Net within hours. The irony was obvious. Warner, owner of its own self-named label, Elektra, Atlantic, and others, was among the most conservative of the labels with regards to online digitizing its music.

The day after it was released, Gnutella was ordered taken down from the Nullsoft website; evidently, calls from Warner demanded that even distant parts of the company not be seen as supporting the Napster phenomenon so explicitly.

"How do you think we make money?" the Warner side asked newcomers AOL and Nullsoft. Because the program's open source license let anyone who wanted to continue to develop Gnutella, several teams of diverse developers stepped up to do so, while Frankel was effectively cut off from any work on his second greatest creation. He was held back by the golden handcuffs. But work on Gnutella continued. Young hackers picked up the task of perfecting Gnutella, and, as with many open source efforts, keeping the project from splintering soon proved hard to manage. Many different groups were developing their own implementations of the code.

Remaining diffuse had its advantages, chief among them being that, by design, the service was a challenging focus for an RIAA lawsuit. In fact Gene Kan, the most prominent post-Nullsoft developer and spokesman for Gnutella, spoke out on every occasion, including before a Congressional committee, and seemed to have no concern about being singled out.

By mid-2000, the list of Napster and Gnutella clones had swollen. Permutations of the programs included Mactella, Bugzilla, Hagelslag, Gnucleus, MyGnut, and Pornster, as well as Spyster, a privacy wake-up call that let users monitor the IP addresses and activities of online traders. These fit nicely beside a rising ecology of Napster parasites, such as Napigator and Open Nap, which let Napster fans stick with the easy-to-use program's protocols while allowing and facilitating the use of different servers outside of Napster control. This would be handy for a number of reasons, such as finding a server with more users, faster rate of service, or musical taste more like one's own. Adam Powell, CEO of Angry Coffee, a site that offered online music tutorials, had been a strong opponent of Napster and the attitude that copying songs without paying was OK. But his attitude changed. "I started really thinking that there may be something wrong with my position," he said. "It's not as simple as '20 million Elvis fans can't be wrong,' but there is something there. Maybe this is just the crudest bludgeon that needs to be shaped into a finer tool, but there is something there and all the screaming about how it's hurting artists isn't going to change anything." Along with his CTO Jeff Burchell, a.k.a. "Toxic" (one of the architects of the Clearstation stock trading service), Powell launched Percolator, which enabled searches of Napster databases from its own Web site. The company was quickly blocked by Napster and sternly warned not to mess around with its system. When it came to protecting its intellectual property, Napster was again clearly bullish.

While Gnutella and the Napster clones proved that it's difficult to kill an idea on the Internet when there are so many who support it, Ian Clarke's Freenet project offered what may be the most permanent challenge to copyright holders and those who would like to put some regulations onto electronic distribution.

One of the most outspoken, and technologically effective, critics of attempts to sabotage progress for the sake of the status quo, Clarke was, in 2000, a twenty-five-year-old Irish programmer whose dedication to free speech led him to write a program that threatened to take the Napster phenomenon to the extreme. Clarke didn't start out with much of a political agenda, and was far from interested in shaking up the music business, *per se*. He grew up in County Meath, Ireland, the son of a sports shop owner. The only boy in his large family not enthralled by soccer, Clark was interested in science from an early age and won awards for high school science projects such as "The Milk Bottle: Friend or Foe." While studying artificial intelligence and computer science at Edinburgh University in Scotland, he began to immerse himself in the Net, an experience that he says led to his hard-line stance on freedom of information.

"I think that information should be free, and I don't think that you should have half measures," said Clarke. His Freenet allowed its users to post and retrieve files with complete anonymity. While potential uses might include the distribution of everything from suppressed political information to kiddy porn, in the wake of Napster, Freenet was heralded by file-trading supporters as the final rebuttal to arguments that copyrighted songs would be controlled by legal or technical force. Clarke himself was proud to boast that while one could spend a lifetime trying to persuade all sides to agree that information should be free—and might get nowhere—by building Freenet he had made arguments futile.

Many were claiming that the structure of the Internet itself made file-sharing applications like Napster and Gnutella inevitable; Clarke went one further and explained that he himself, as well as his peers, were products of the Internet revolution. "I was lucky enough to grow up using the Internet over the last five years," Clarke said. "I really think that my philosophical and intellectual positions are forged by the Internet more than anything else. Certainly more than anyone that I've spoken to." A statement like that recalled the pronouncements of a *Wired* editor and author, Kevin Kelly, who throughout the '90s had warned that, though e-mail represented a new flowering of human communication, those who weren't using it couldn't understand it. Immersing himself in the exciting online exchange of ideas and growing cooperative efforts such as the open-source movement convinced Clarke that trying to own information was not only impractical, it was counter-productive.

"I think that there is almost a new Renaissance going on, but unfortunately it's limited to a few people," Clarke said. "The reason why hackers laugh at all of this paranoia is because it's totally on the wrong side of the Renaissance. People's intellectual development in terms of ideas and philosophies are just going into overdrive on the Internet, and those that can't afford it, or are just not interested, are being left behind." If innovation was to continue at Internet speed, the pretense of keeping track of and administering the ownership of ideas would have to stop. Although Clarke was neither politically or socially extreme—he was in most ways clean-cut and business-minded—the tendencies of copyright to encourage monopoly was, for him, proof enough that it must end.

"If there was a cancer in capitalism it would be monopoly—and I don't mean the game," said Clarke. "It demonstrates why capitalism alone is not sufficient. It does provide fertile ground for monopolies to form, and monopolies end up hurting everyone but themselves; Microsoft, of course being the ever-present example." Clarke's soft-spoken but cutting critiques of the status quo led the press to brand him an anarchist, or as *Time* magazine perhaps more aptly put it, an "infoanarchist."

Freenet modeled itself on its home, the Internet, and followed a P2P protocol, distributing the workload among everyone running a server, so that there was no central repository that could be attacked and no one person who could be bribed or cajoled into taking down the system. Clarke liked to tell reporters that even if someone put a gun to his head, he couldn't take Freenet down. Pieces of information, particularly if they were in high demand, would be copied and distributed through the network, protecting them from removal and making them easy to access.

After he had the initial idea for Freenet, working away in his room above the dark streets of Edinburgh, Clarke ran some simulations that proved to him that his hypotheses would work. After posting the idea on the Net, Clarke attracted help to develop the network. Soon there were twenty-five developers laboring to build it, none of whom Clarke had ever met or even spoken with on the phone. Freeing information had no business model, and after graduation, Clarke supported himself by moving to London and working at an e-commerce firm. As word of Freenet made the rounds, Clarke was contacted by Net-savvy Hollywood lawyers Ken Hertz and Fred Goldring, advisers working with Rob Kramer, former CEO of the digital animation studio Moving Pixels. Together with Clarke, the Hollywood insiders hatched a company called Uprizer, conceived as a way for artists to make money in a world in which the power of copyright, as well as that of big record labels, had been neutered. Clarke quit his prosaic London day job and followed the beckoning lights to work in Santa Monica. Uprizer was one of the most-talked-about, least-understood projects on the Net, and its owners wanted it that way. Vigorously secretive while working the conference circuit with his outspoken critiques of copyright, Clarke seemed to have little time to work on the project. At any rate, it remained veiled in obscurity well into 2001.

"It's easier to enjoy music when you think that you're making a difference. I believe that I'm making a difference for the better, and I think other people will realize that in time. If you look at the music industry at the moment, the people that do the worst are the artists, with the consumers coming in a close second." Clarke pointed to a speech by Courtney Love and the theory that even famous artists weren't doing so well under the current system. "So in some senses almost any change will be for the good."

Because the development of Freenet essentially trumped all technical attempts to stop unauthorized distribution, by the June 2000 MP3 summit, at which an interview with Clarke by journalist Bruce Haring was a keynote event, piracy seemed to be less a point of outrage or outlaw swagger and more an accepted fact of life to be accounted for and minimized by those doing business on the Net. Speaker after speaker warned the labels that they must face the issue squarely: they needed to somehow provide extra value to attract music listeners who might otherwise trade freely. Whether through quality assurance, depth of user experience, respected seal of quality,

or all of the above topped with a competitive price, many urged labels to save themselves. Clarke, who had no love for the current big
labels, drove home the urgency facing the industry by saying: "if you
sell water in the desert and it starts to rain, you need to develop a different model. Part of a capitalist society is that things change; people
go out of business all the time. It's up to them, [record labels] need to
adapt, but I'm not sure they're capable of making the kinds of
changes they need to survive."

One record executive who was certainly nimble and willing to make
changes was Edgar Bronfman Jr., an heir to the Seagram's empire,
whose career had included shedding great portions of the company in
moves that proved much shrewder in the long run than they were perceived at the time and boosted revenues and company value. He was
also known as someone who valued music, highly, and especially got a
kick out of seeing a song sell. This interest took a personal turn when
he cowrote a song on the *Titanic* soundtrack, "To Love You More,"
which *Gavin* reported sold 1.2 million copies. While Bronfman agreed
to sell Universal to French multimedia group Vivendi, thus giving up
all but a quarter role in the company's online musical future, in May
Bronfman delivered a passionate call to arms against online traders
who didn't respect the company's intellectual property. In fact he declaration was more than passionate: in many points its lack of consis-
tency and strange martial metaphors verged on hysterical. In San Jose,
California, for the Real Conference 2000, in which he announced a
Universal joint project with streaming giant RealNetworks, Bronfman
addressed the assembled crowd of techies like an irate boss, used to
getting his way, basically threatening to shut down the Internet if it
didn't do what he wanted. He called for the industry to move faster
into the Web but to remain steadfast against pirating.

"We now live in an era in which a few clicks of your mouse will
make it possible for you to summon every book ever written in any
language, every movie ever made, every television show ever produced, and every piece of music ever recorded," he said, a little pre-
maturely, adding that music was on the leading edge of this revolution
and was the first product to show the need to protect intellectual

property rights. "For all of us, 'property' rights are well understood and universally accepted. You own a home. You own a car. They're yours—they belong to you. They are your property. Well, your ideas belong to you, too. And intellectual property is property, period."

"If intellectual property is not protected—across the board, in every case, with no exceptions and no sophistry about a changing world— what will happen? Intellectual property will suffer the fate of the buffalo." Ignoring the durability of great unprotected works from The Bible and Plato to Shakespeare and Bach, Bronfman added that "the great ferment of works and ideas, including your own, if taken at will and without restraint, have no chance of surviving any better than did the buffalo."

Bronfman said that, to make sure that the Internet didn't attempt to develop separately in a world apart from the rule of civilization, he would stage a military invasion, of sorts. "I am warring against the culture of the Internet, threatening to depopulate Silicon Valley as I move a Roman legion or two of Wall Street lawyers to litigate in Bellevue and San Jose. I have moved those lawyers—or some of them—but I have done so, and will continue to do so—not to attack the Internet and its culture but for its benefit and to protect it. *For its benefit.*" He was warring, but not attacking, depopulating but protecting. No wonder the soft-spoken, but rational-sounding views of Ian Clarke seemed so appealing in contrast.

Sandwiched between the absurd bluster, Bronfman not only outlined where he intended to take Universal, but also made some reasonable points. He accused Napster of taking advantage of "each person's least admirable qualities" by encouraging Net users to download for free what they had stated "time and again" that they would pay for. His outline of Universal's Internet strategy was fairly comprehensive, if somewhat overshadowed by his threats. The plan was four-pronged. Universal would create, with partners like InterTrust and Real, a secure system for musical delivery that would be "far richer" than the uncivilized one proposed by MP3.com and Napster by including album art, liner notes, and possibly chats with artists. With Sony, a subscription service would be launched. He also called for an educational effort to teach that the Internet must exist within the rule of law that took civilization hundreds of years to develop.

Bronfman's fourth prong was enforcement. "Technology exists that can trace every Internet download and tag every file," he said. "These tools make it possible to identify those who are using the Internet to improperly and illegally acquire music and other copyrighted information. While adhering to the principle of respect for individual privacy, we fully intend to exploit technology to protect the property which rightfully belongs to its owners." While letting that ambitious project sink in, he outlined Universal's recent successes on the legal front, which included a suit against MP3.com and Napster, among others.

The tone of battle reflected the stakes that copyright owners felt were in play. To survive they would have to fight, as Hilary Rosen put it, the trend of file sharing to "reduce the value of music to free." Or, as in the case with MP3.com, the trend of others profiting from songs owned by labels without first paying for licensing. On the side of the labels was the Digital Millennium Copyright Act, a piece of legislation that was supported by the Clinton administration and crafted by senators such as Orrin Hatch of Utah, which many believed overstepped its bounds by strongly criminalizing acts like disabling copyright protection software, even if it were to access something a consumer already owned. Eventually, even Hatch would come to question the DMCA's wisdom, especially when it was being expressed by the RIAA. As the singer-songwriter of his own Mormon folk music, Hatch was no doubt aware that he might benefit from distribution outside the vulgar greedy clutches of the recording industry.

As for Napster, newly appointed CEO Hank Barry wasn't sitting still. The first item on his agenda was finding someone who had the legal savvy and persuasiveness to fight the expensive, high-powered lawyers that the RIAA was sending to court. Topping the list: David Boies, the star attorney who built the Department of Justice's winning case against tech giant Microsoft. It was Boies's sons who convinced him that the Napster case was worth his interest. The Microsoft case notwithstanding, Boies was not particularly interested in either the Net or popular music. What he was interested in was fighting important cases, and the more he heard, the more he was convinced that this was very important. "Here you have a new technology—in terms of peer-to-peer sharing of information—and if that technology is going to work, you must allow people to provide central indexes of the data. Somebody's got to maintain those indexes," he told *Wired* magazine. "I mean, it's just like a newspaper that publishes classified ads. You've got to have a place where people can go who want to participate in that kind of activity. And if you, in effect, impose on the directory-service provider liability to investigate, monitor, and control what the users are doing, it is very difficult to see how that kind of technology is ever going to work."

With the case in progress, Boies joined the team in June, and set to work arguing against the injunction facing Napster. The work took a harrowing, frenzied pace, and surely put Boies and his team through its paces. His reasoning developed into three parts solid argument and one part something that most legal experts viewed as a distraction: the notion that by blocking developing markets, the recording industry had lost its authority to claim copyrights. That argument brought a lot of attention, coming as it did on the heels of the Microsoft antitrust success.

But the main points of defense to fight the RIAA's suit were that sharing music was legal for consumers not engaged in profit-making, based on the 1992 Audio Home Recording Act. The defense argued secondly that, as when Sony was sued by the film industry for its video recorder, there were plenty of significant legitimate uses for Napster, and thirdly, that as an ISP, Napster couldn't be held responsible for listings that appeared in its directory.

Unfortunately for the Napster team, when the hearing convened on July 26 in Federal District Court of San Francisco, Judge Patel did not agree. With any of it. She was clearly upset by the Napster program, which she referred to as a "site," and had no qualms interrupting Boies whenever she felt his arguments strayed from common sense. After listening to Boies's arguments for about ten minutes, Patel stopped the attorney, and wanted to know one thing: If Napster offered so many compelling uses outside of trading copyrighted songs, why would an order to suspend the trading of those songs force the company out of business. "Isn't that inconsistent?" she asked, also arguing that it was piracy that drove Napster, first and foremost.

"If you design a site to enable infringement, you can't stand by and claim you don't know what's going on." Patel was more inclined to listen to the plea from RIAA attorney Russell Frackman, who, after describing the litany of harm that Napster was doing its clients, implored that "your honor has the ability to nip this in the bud." Patel agreed, and ordered Napster to remove any infringing files by the week's end, issuing what looked like a death sentence for the nascent company. Because Napster had no way, or at least no intention of, watching out for unauthorized songs on its service, the ruling would be a mortal blow. Besides, of course, it was copyrighted music that was drawing so many people to the program.

Once Patel's decision was delivered, Napster filed an immediate appeal, to be considered two days later by the Ninth Circuit Court of Appeals. In a message to Napster users, streamed live across the Net, Barry and Fanning vowed to continue the fight. In the meantime, a rush of users swarmed to the Net and their Napster programs, hoping to gather all the music they could before the curtain fell. Many pundits predicted that the industry might have won the battle but could anticipate losing the war: Gnutella or Freenet would rise to replace Napster, and by squashing one main offender, the RIAA would let a hundred more rise in its place. That didn't stop the industry from gloating over the victory.

Two days later, a shocking reprise was delivered for Fanning and company: the three-judge team at the Ninth Circuit agreed that the case warranted further reflection and overruled Patel's injunction, giving Napster until August 18 to present arguments why the injunction shouldn't hold, after which there would be a Ninth Circuit appeal hearing. Napster had, the judges said, raised substantial questions about the "both the merits and the form of the injunction." Both sides, one rejoicing, the other "disappointed," affirmed their belief that it was the novelty, as well the importance, of the Internet issues that led the panel to believe the case merited further consideration than Patel had offered. A hearing to have the injunction reinstated was set for the first week of October. A full trial over copyright violations was not expected until mid-2001. The publicity from the case, the sense of a still-looming showdown, and the simple continuation of an explosive growth pattern meant that Napster was left clearly more popular than before the suit began, and its base of users and supporters seemed to swell. For the moment though, the community wasn't helping Michael Robertson much. On September 6, Judge Jed S. Rakoff delivered his ruling that MP3.com would have to pay Universal Music $25,000 for each of the CDs it had copied to stream to consumers who also owned those discs. It looked as though MP3.com would be forced to pay Universal somewhere between $118 million and $250 million. While noting that he could have set a penalty as high as $150,000 per disc, Rakoff admitted that he hoped the penalty would sting. "There is no doubt in the court's mind that the potential for huge profits in the rapidly expanding world of the Internet is the lure that tempted an otherwise generally responsible company like MP3.com to break the law and that will also tempt others to do so if too low a level is set for the statutory damages in this case," Rakoff said. He also seemed to make an allusion to the Napster case when he noted that "some companies operating in the area of the Internet" seemed to believe that "because their technology is somewhat novel, they are somehow immune from the ordinary applications of laws."

The ruling was based, as Robertson feared, on each CD violation. It was the largest copyright violation in history, hitting MP3.com with a crippling fee. Robertson, who felt he wasn't hurting the labels at all, called it an outrageous amount, "considering they didn't incur one penny of damages. Everything we did with our system was designed to get people to buy more CDs. That's why it was a real travesty to have that fine."

The judgment also justified, to Robertson, his never-ending need to demo his product at every possible occasion. While this habit was a minor point of derision among those who followed the technology closely enough to understand its nuances, Robertson believed, rightly,

that he was fighting an uphill battle against those who didn't understand what his products did and had confusingly lumped him together
with Napster. (Not that his firebrand rebellious posturing at the first
half of MP3.com's life hadn't helped that categorization.) Robertson
was consistent in his attempts to reach out to those who were new to
the Net.

"We have to be on a continuing, call it education, call it evangelist,
call it salesman, role, call it what you will. It's a very dynamic changing industry and it's important to let people know what's going on."
He said the new Net-based services he offered were radically different from the switch to, say, online book ordering from a usual trip to
Waldenbooks. "We're talking about radically fundamentally changing
how they buy their music, how much music they buy, how they listen
to their music. Amazon isn't changing how you read books; we are
changing how you listen to music, where you listen to it, what music
you listen to, and how artists get paid. That kind of radical change, I
would suggest, makes the music industry the most impacted by the
Internet of any industry in the world."

These new models didn't appear from nowhere. Robertson had
been trying all year to develop innovative programs to stay ahead of
industry trends. To address the point of changing how artists (Alanis
Morissette notwithstanding) were paid, MP3.com launched "Payback
for Playback" in November 1999, a system that distributed a million
dollars per month among all the artists on the site, according to how
popular they were. Even though the money wasn't guaranteed to last,
it was meant as a move in the direction of a TV-like model where actors are paid indirectly through advertising fees, and made success
stories out of MP3.com artists, something the company needed desperately. In a move that he said promoted industry transparency,
Robertson posted all bands' earnings on their Web pages.

"There's this big craziness murkiness fuzziness, crazy accounting,
we wanted to rip the top off it, and let anyone in the world audit our
numbers every day," Robertson said. "We were trying to put a new
spin on it all, by putting it all in the open . . . . Secrets are bad
things—they usually mean that somebody's getting screwed, and if

you don't know who's getting screwed it's probably you. It was controversial, but I think the benefit far outweighs the concern."

In May 2000, following up on ideas espoused by Internet theorists like Todd Rundgren and Jim Griffin, Robertson began to experiment with various subscription models. The first, launched in May, let patrons subscribe to individual artists, or labels, at fees set by the artist, splitting the take fifty-fifty with the artist. In June, MP3.com tested another idea as it rolled out a classical music channel and let users pay a monthly fee for access to everything offered in the genre.

Emusic, taking a pounding from the popularity of Napster, also started a subscription service that month, letting users download anything on the site for $19.95 a month, less if bought for a full year. Emusic spokesman Steve Curry believed that the company was presenting a workable alternative that consumers and artists would ultimately embrace over the confusing, costly, and intrusive digital rights management systems.

The subscription model allowed Emusic to raise money in interesting new ways. A deal with Hewlett-Packard was announced that committed the computer maker to a minimum of $3 million worth of Emusic subscriptions, to be bundled with new computers and CD burners.

Entertainment consolidation was big news in 2000 and 2001. It's impossible to talk about mergers without mentioning the joining of Time Warner with America Online, a monster that would dwarf all other media conglomerates, with a combined $34.2 billion in annual revenue. AOL Time Warner's brands included CompuServe, Netscape, CNN, *Sports Illustrated*, ICQ, AOL Instant Messenger, AOL MovieFone, TBS, TNT, Cartoon Network, Digital City, Warner Music Group, Spinner, Winamp, *Fortune*, AOL.com, *Entertainment Weekly*, and Looney Tunes.

It also had Nullsoft, creator of Winamp and Gnutella. But as the pressure from all sides began to take its toll on creativity, Nullsoft was soon to lose two of its pioneers, Rob Lord and Ian Rogers.

"AOL is really pretty hands-off with us at Nullsoft," said Lord in April 2000, a few months before he left. He insisted that the only time Nullsoft got in trouble with its new owners was over the

Gnutella launch. He believed that AOL, enormously powerful while less hampered than any other major by old baggage, would push the online music agenda. "I believe that AOL stands the biggest chance of really making Internet music happen. Between mass reach, mass usage, and access to all this content, for AOL it's really a matter of coordination more than anything else. We want Winamp.com to be essentially a portal where you choose what you want, and we're not directing you at all." But a certain amount of simpatico didn't prevent Lord from having reservations about his parent company. "I don't doubt for a minute that this is the biggest organized culture pusher that the world has ever seen, and it's terrifying in its vastness and its ability to change ideas."

The mixed feelings, evidently, were more than mutual, and Lord was let go in June, the result of conflicting visions about where to go in an online music world that took Napster and Gnutella as givens. Ian Rogers believed that Lord was a scapegoat, singled out as the voice of dissent in order make way for the company to come around to his ideas without losing face. Rogers decided to leave with Lord. As a parting gesture, the pair painted a slew of signs featuring the company mascot, a llama, inside a big red heart. Underneath, Lord wrote "We didn't get into this 'space' cuz we're internet gold seeking cockos. We're legitimate nihilistic media terrorists as history will no doubt canonize us."

On June 9, the pair decorated the AOL San Francisco offices with the posters and left. The four original members of the Winamp team, Frankel, Pepper, Lord, and Rogers were now apart, just as the company was asking them to accept new compromises.

In July, AOL announced its own, corporate-sanctioned move to develop what it hoped would be another Napster, waiting to step in and work legally. "AOL plus InterTrust equals legal Napster," said Talal Shamoon, InterTrust's vice president. "Consumers could be billed by the month for what they consume." The InterTrust system, which was also embraced by Universal and BMG, would facilitate the collection fees from subscribers, who could then be billed in a variety of ways. By going with AOL, InterTrust was guaranteed a route to ubiquity: distribution on the free AOL installation discs that threatened to take over the universe. The first application was to be a new version of Winamp equipped with the company's right's management software, or "Digibox secure containers."

The announcement, and the general embrace of "digital rights management" tools such as InterTrust had its fair share of critics, even from within industry circles. "InterTrust is a security tool which seems to ignore completely what consumers want to do," asserted Ken Hertz. "What the record companies are trying to do is create systems that replicate their business model in a virtual world; the problem is that kids don't behave the way they do in the real world in the virtual world. They'll sell you a digital file that behaves just like a record: you can keep it, you can play it, you can have it, if you can give it to a friend he can keep it, he can play it, he can have it, but you can't anymore, unless you want to pay again. Who's going to do that? In my opinion encryption seems to completely ignore the reality of where the technology goes." The plan didn't sit well with the boy wonders at Nullsoft either, who were left feeling as if their baby had been sold out, which of course it had. It's a cliché at many Web companies that their greatest capital gets up and walks out the door every night. The trouble for AOL was that the remaining Winamp team, while they were generally coming back every day, didn't want to play by the corporate rules. AOL was all about playing by the book, and that seemed to stick in the craw of the freedom lovers, however obvious this should have been.

Also upsetting for Frankel was the order not to work on Gnutella, his naughty baby, taken away by the corporate truant officers. In an online diary (he only allows the entries to be printed in full), one could tell the strain was getting to him:

7/30/00

Had a great b-day party for Allison last night.

On to a different subject.

It really sucks when you do something cool and let it out into the world, and then get your hands cut off from it.

Example:
http://music.cnet.com/music/0–1652424–7–2375754.html
(the whole thing), and in the "CNET's MP3 Buzz" section on the right side, things like "Can't Get Enough of Gene Kan? Listen to Gnutella's creator . . ." and "Our sources have been complaining of slow service and interrupted downloads from Gnutella over the last few days, leading us to speculate that Gnutella's recent surge of traffic is too much for the service to bear. We're hoping that its many developers figure out what's going on. "

Gnutella's many developers? Funny this is, the Gnutella network out there is mostly running (according to our crawler) the good ol' Gnutella that we made months ago. Many developers? Hah. And we know just how to make it scale a lot better, and we are in a position where we could get most of the clients upgraded in a matter of a few days, and it would all be good. But we can't (right now).

I don't want this to be taken the wrong way, I'm not asking for more credit here. I just hate it when other people get credit for something they didn't do. Gene Kan, I can't blame, I mean what would you do if you had that chance . . . ugh.

that didn't make too much sense, I have a hangover.

Others on the team also seemed to have been feeling the pressure. Tom Pepper's entry in his diary on May 6 said "getting more and more tired of hearing the importance of capitalism, and get a little more tired each day of defending the Nullsoft Way(tm). A little episode last week made me perk up an eye that people outside our camp seem interested in promoting some of what we've been doing.

It's interesting to see the effects of some creeping factionalism." At least they still had their cars, swimming pools, and fun cabanas to console themselves with. For AOL, if not yet Time Warner, the system showed how seriously the company was taking the Net, and the way corporate heads saw online music developing: fully padlocked.

* * *

Not all players at the labels were as gung ho about lawsuits and military metaphors as Bronfman, the Universal CEO. Whereas he was lost in a maze of metaphors, EMI's Ted Cohen and vice president Jay Sammit tried for a more realistic assessment of their label's situation. "The question isn't: Do we put David Bowie's catalog up on the Internet?" said Ted Cohen. "That decision was already made for us by other people, it's already there." The real question, he believed, was how to create an environment in which people would rather pay David Bowie for his work than steal it from him.

In July, EMI chose 100 albums by its artists to release online, using the Windows Media format because of its digital rights management abilities and making the songs available using Liquid Audio, among other options, which protected the files from unlimited copying. Cohen's boss, Jay Sammit, head of interactive media at EMI, said in a prepared statement, "About a year ago, we still had a lot of Luddites in the music industry. That day is long gone and there's a great market out there." He didn't mention what happened to those Luddites.

The experiment was far from successful, however, due to poor promotion. Its navigation was hard to follow once a consumer landed at a participating site; few people bought the high-priced singles. Cohen was contrite. "We concentrated on working with our retailers so that technologically they were up to speed. We believed that they would understand how to best merchandise, because they're merchandisers. The record stores, Tower, Wherehouse, Transworld, and Virgin know how to do displays in their stores, and they know how to put things on the front page of their Web site. But you had to basically do a search to find the stuff. [The accounts] were just so worried that it worked technologically that they forgot about the marketing aspect. They worried more about what the customer experience would be then about how they would actually find it. It's got to be: I want it, click on it, and I have it. It's got to be like buying on Amazon."

As far as other labels went, most expressed initial shock, even out-rage, at EMI's timing, but then followed up shortly with their own systems. Cohen said, "We put our hundred albums up . . . and I was getting all kinds of grief from people at other labels, going 'Why did you do this now? Why didn't you wait?' We got a call from Universal asking why we were doing it. Two weeks later, they did it. Was it a question of why did we do it, or was it why did we beat them by two weeks? It's just that we got our stuff out there before they did."

He joked about how difficult it had been to actually pay for and download a song, and counted thirteen steps a consumer had to fol-low just in order to get one song legally. "Alcoholics Anonymous has a twelve-step program. For digital downloads we have a thirteen-step program. We want you to be even more patient." Despite the wise-cracks, Cohen was reassuring that the process would get smoother. "They're all learning. Our goal is to make legitimate music easier and easier to get, and make illegitimate music harder and harder to get. The EMI philosophy right now is that we want our stuff on as many places as possible, as long as we know who the people are, and if they're using our content to 'make a lot of money,' we want some-thing back."

Cohen believed that the company was putting together all the pieces. He defended the industry against many of the charges of not being willing to try new things, but described artists hoping for better contracts as waiting to exploit the label's weak position. "I really do believe the labels *get it* more than anyone gives them credit for. Situa-tions occur continuously where the record companies go to the artists and say we want to do such and such, and the artists are there saying 'my record company doesn't do this and my label doesn't do that.' The reality is that they view it as an opportunity to renegotiate their deal. You say you want to do downloads, and they'll say 'Oh well, that's not specifically covered in my contract, I want to go back and renegotiate my whole record deal.' Or, 'Why would I want to do that if I could do it with Artist Direct.' We come with opportunities, and the artists and managers in frequent cases view it as an opportunity to reopen some issue that has nothing to do with what we're asking them about."

While Cohen was back inside the heart of the industry in his position at EMI, a rumored half million dollars a year was his reward for coming back after a very successful career as a consultant. After helping Amazon repurpose its bookselling experience to build a music site, Cohen became highly sought out as someone with feet planted both in the Web and music businesses. He helped music news site Webnoize develop what would be a key yearly conference. Eventually he was put on retainer for twenty-five organizations, including both Napster and RIAA, at the same time. Cohen said he was "advising Napster on being 'label friendly' while explaining to RIAA that this was a whole new model, and there might be some way to get [Napster] to play nice." Whatever his personal skill in navigating both sides, Cohen was not able to bring them together. "As it turned out, Napster was having too much fun being the outlaw. So at a certain point I had to bail."

Cohen commanded a great deal of respect in the music world, where he'd been an active advocate of innovation for years. But he seemed to resent some in the industry who claimed credit for ideas that have been tossed around freely for some time. "The industry people say to me 'gee, have you ever heard Jim Griffin's philosophy on ubiquity of music, and streaming everywhere?' . . . Jim's done a much better job proselytizing that environment than I have, because it's become known as 'the Jim Griffin philosophy.' In 1993 at Digital Hollywood at the Beverly Hilton, I gave a speech in which I said that I've got three thousand CDs in my living room. I said here I am, I'm up here on a panel today; tomorrow I leave for New York. Tomorrow I'll pick nine or ten of them to put in my CD wallet to take with me. I said I would trade ownership of my 3,000 CDs for access to my 3,000 CDs wherever I go."

Regardless of whose idea a celestial jukebox was, the fact that one of its chief advocates was in a position of power at a major label was clearly a step toward some kind of reconciliation between the music industry and online music consumers. It even started looking like there might be room for some of the bad boy online companies. Sales didn't seem to be so affected by Napster use, although an important new marketplace was arguably being, if not ignored, at least not openly exploited.

Ken Hertz said, "The marketing people are chomping at the bit to take advantage of these opportunities, instead of towing the company line and circling the wagons to defend the existing business model. The marketing guys are like 'hey guys, great, I'm sure when you crunch your numbers and look at your projections we're all at risk, but guess what? I've got 20 million Napster users and I want them to know that this record is coming out."

The new attitudes of record execs were born in part by a late realization in many quarters of the industry that online music is much more of an opportunity than a threat. On August 25, the RIAA reported that, "The number of full-length CDs manufacturers shipped to the U.S. market is at an all-time high, growing 6.0 percent from this time last year, totaling an impressive 420 million units in just the first six months of 2000. This puts CDs at 86 percent of the total music purchasing market. Moreover, market momentum continues to climb as the dollar value of CD product grew 9.9 percent from this time last year to nearly $5.7 billion, which suggests once again, that consumer demand for music in the form of a CD remains the mainstay. The growth can be attributed in part to an impressive number of first-quarter release successes, including Britney Spears, 'N Sync, and Eminem."

For artists, picking sides was difficult and knowing whom to believe was harder still. King Crimson guitarist Robert Fripp, an industry stalwart, known for his no-nonsense approach to business, attempted to sort his thoughts in an orderly manner, an ended up with a piece that appeared on his Web site in almost poetic form:

> *The RIAA represents the interests of the majors.*
> *The interests of the majors are contrary to the interests of*
> *artists.*

The RIAA does not represent the interests of artists, and to suggest this is fundamentally dishonest.
The RIAA does not have the aim of making music available to the listening community.
Napster does make music available to the listening community.
The RIAA does not represent artists.
Napster does not represent artists either.
The good news: Napster demonstrates the importance which people attach to having music in their lives.
This is legitimate: music is a need in our lives.
The bad news: the public at large is prepared to act illegitimately to serve this legitimate impulse.
The challenge: to legitimize, validate & redeem the clearly demonstrated want, wish, need & intent to share with others music which we value."

8

OUT OF THE BOTTLE AND INTO YOUR EAR

At the helm of a $6 billion company, RealNetworks founder Rob Glaser was in a position to see the wheels of power spinning, even to be one of those wheels. As Napster headed to court to battle the RIAA, he expressed a dim view of the influence of the labels and film studios in setting the online legal standards. "If you look at any particular aspect of the political process, and the legislative process," he said, "it's basically just a few wires short of being an ATM at this point. That's a terrible corrupting thing for society as a whole, and it tends to bias towards established industries, and they are the ones who have the (often errantly perceived) interests in preserving the status quo."

But if the arena was tilted, then the sheer popularity of file sharing meant that its millions of users had become a political counterweight. "The fact that the Internet is a community does change the debate and does affect the outcome," Glaser said. "The fact that there are now tens of millions of users of a service like Napster or 150 million RealPlayer users does have an immutable and deep impact on these processes, even though they may be imperfect because of certain industries having huge lobbying apparatuses in Washington, D.C." Glaser believed that striking the right balance between the interests of consumers, industries, and the enabling of new technologies was "more art than science," particularly with ephemeral product forms that threw a wrench into agreements on the line between personal use and nonpersonal use, fair use and infringement, and between broadcasting and distribution. "There are all of these traditional things that had fairly well-understood meanings that the interactive digital age and the Internet completely blurs the lines of, so that there's no practical alternative but engaging." And the engagement was on, and all concerned eyes turned to the courts.

Orrin Hatch, for one, was paying attention. Though he was one of the drafters of the Digital Millennium Copyright Act, by late 2000 the senator from Utah seemed less confident that the act had been as fair as it should have been, given that the RIAA, as well as the Motion Picture Association of America, were relying so heavily on scaring developing companies with potentially eviscerating lawsuits. He described to the press incidents in which he was hoping to resolve copyright disputes with the file-sharing company Scour, only to find the industry associations were already suing. "That rubbed me the wrong way," he said, though "it comes as no surprise that the recording industry has used litigation to scare off the venture capitalists to put their money elsewhere. They are targeting small, under-funded companies who can't afford to fight them (in order) to establish a strong case law in this area." Those interests were taking on just such an under-funded venture when they took on Napster.

The ornate rooms of the U.S. Ninth Circuit Court of Appeals in San Francisco presented an image of federal power, a line traced, architecturally, back to the glory of Rome, supplemented with a few gilded, baroque flourishes—a far cry from the workaday city courthouse. Outside those marble-and-tile halls, on the cool sunny morning of October 2, 2000, a lengthening row of press and observers was lining up, exchanging knowing smiles and semi-competitive glances.

As the personally and professionally interested waited, black cars jerked to the sidewalk and unloaded their passengers, the ready-to-spar representatives of the entertainment power structure as it moved into the information age. Hilary Rosen, dressed in a flashy orange suit that contrasted sharply with the staid clothing of her legal team, looked around, smiled quickly, and walked inside. Another group pulled up, and Napster CEO Hank Barry, David Boies, and Shawn Fanning, surrounded by their PR and legal team, walked through the crowd, past the metal detectors, and up the stairs to the silent, impassive courtroom.

Taking their seats above the packed house was the three-judge panel, Circuit Judge Mary Schroeder, Circuit Judge Richard Paez, and Senior Circuit Judge Robert Beezer. Seventy places, out of the room's 120 seats, had been taken by the teams of the opposing sides, their friends, and family. The other fifty seats were offered to press. There was the almost giddy sense that news was about to be made, a feeling that was barely contained by the ceremony. The judges would hear the appeal from Judge Patel's granting of a preliminary injunction to force Napster to prevent the sharing of copyrighted files, which Napster argued would force it to shut down. While a win here for the underdog would not be a guarantee of survival, it would grant more time, and time was definitely on Napster's side. With such an exponential growth rate, Napster use was becoming established just like Israeli "facts on the ground." If there were already 30 million users, many of them quite fanatical, it was hard to see them going away. The reality that the Napster community was reaching over into AOL-size numbers, and the possibility that someone messing with that group would hit a nerve that that could spill over into even political effects, would only increase. Less tied to the "ATM" that Glaser saw in the legislative process, the courtroom was a key battleground. Even during a short hearing, the precision of focus granted by two smart lawyers arguing their cases would hopefully shed light on some of the issues, and the formality and ritual meant that confusing hype and marketing language from either side would be discouraged.

David Boies was first to take the floor, and he tried to set a high bar establishing what the RIAA needed to prove, and the court accept, for an injunction. "The plaintiffs in this case ask this court to do several things that no appellate court has done in the history of copyright," Boies said dramatically. "First, they ask this court to hold a company liable for contributory or vicarious infringement, when the direct infringer is not engaged in commercial activity, and does not have a commercial relationship with the contributory infringement." The worry in the courtroom, or in some cases the anticipation of *schadenfreude*, was that the judges here would smack down Boies's arguments, or cut him off dismissively as Patel had, bringing down the hero of the Microsoft case. As the court continued to listen respectfully, Boies seemed to pick up some confidence. He reminded the court that, in the Sony Betamax case when the videotape recorder first appeared (the case had been argued in this same court), the technology was found to be infringing, but the ruling was later struck down by the Supreme Court. Napster, Boies argued, was supplying a technology capable of a commercially significant noninfringing use—the key point that saved Sony in its 1984 case versus the movie industry, *Sony v. Universal City Studios*. He also asserted that unless the court found that sharing music by consumers was illegal, the case had no basis. Napster, as an Internet Service Provider, would also have to be found liable for the infringing activity of its users when it couldn't know what its users were doing and when it had suspended service when infringement was brought to its attention, as with Metallica traders. "The plaintiff asks this court to reach each one of those four unprecedented holdings, and this court must reach each of those to find liability," Boies said.

Judge Paez took advantage of a pause to speak, but instead of a rebuke, his was an invitation to continue, a friendly segue to further argument. "There's never been another case like this before, has there?" he asked. Boies said that yes, he thought there was. "The Sony case had a new technology. Sony advertised that technology, sold that technology for purposes of making copies of copyrighted works. There was no doubt that the primary purpose was to copy copyrighted material . . . . This court, in an opinion that was ultimately reversed by the Supreme Court, found that that constituted contributory infringement." Judge

Schroeder suggested that Patel's reasoning seemed sound when she said it wasn't fair use when someone made music anonymously available to anyone in the world.

Boies evaded that argument by asserting that in the Sony case, despite the huge, almost exclusive, use of VCRs for duplicating copyrighted shows, the court had ruled that if there was reasonable, if small, noninfringing use, then that outweighed the possible massive violation. "They talked about the significance of one movie that was not copyrighted, *My Man Godfrey*, and one television show, the *Mr. Rogers Show*, that gave permission for use, and that was significant." It was important to recognize these uses, especially in a new technology, because the number of noninfringing uses increased all the time. "You can't take a snapshot" to judge a developing tool because then you'll stop the technology before it can fully develop. This set up a lengthy discussion, driven by Judge Beezer, about whether Napster was a service or a technology, and which part of its functionality fell under which rubric. If the Napster *service* could be shut down, the solely *mechanical* portions, such as the servers, would not be affected. With this, Boies's twenty minutes were nearly up, and he reserved some time for his rebuttal.

With an upbeat manner that seemed to slip between plaintive tones and confidence, RIAA lawyer Russell Frackman took the floor, eager to dispel the notion that the Napster case had anything to do with Sony. "Napster is nothing like the VCR in Sony. Napster really is and was designed to be the gatekeeper of this entire system. They were going to 'control' the user's environment," he said, quoting from some notes that Napster cocreator Sean Parker had written, which were presented as evidence in the circuit court. Riffing on Beezer's train of questioning, Frackman said that it was only Napster's servers that could reasonably be described as equivalent to the mechanical videotape recorder. The rest was a service, programmed to infringe. "We're not talking about a technology, we're talking about a business plan," he said. Did Napster or its employees have their fingerprints on the data, Judge Beezer asked, were they responsible for the songs? Frackman said that no, in the sense of actually putting the material on, but in the sense of being the cause for that material to be distributed, they certainly did have fingerprints all over it. "Their fingerprints you can't find because Napster doesn't want you to find them," Frackman said. "There isn't a case around that says you have to know every single piece of copyrighted material that you're contributing to the infringement of. We sent them notice of 12,000 copyrights, they're still on Napster."

He then went on to say that it was Napster's fault if its technology, which he didn't find that groundbreaking, had to be shut down. "No one can get that material without Napster using its *server* for this *service*," he said, and if the company couldn't run one without the other it was the fault of its creators. "Whether or not Napster chooses to suspend what they're doing is not relevant . . . . If they have created a situation where they either choose not to or cannot continue operation because of the massive infringement involved, then we as the copyright owners are entitled to injunctive relief expressly permitted in the copyright act."

It was the RIAA that was getting grilled this time. When Frackman compared the Napster case to an earlier suit that forced swap meet owners to accept responsibility for pirated works traded in their domain, Schroeder, who presided over that case, said that the cases weren't at all the same, because it was much easier for a swap meet owner to watch over the goods being traded, much harder when millions of electronic files were involved. Beezer wanted to know about works that the RIAA members didn't control. "I find this very troubling," he said, that "you may have given notice of a couple of thousand works, but what of the millions of other works out there and what of the legitimate releases and fair uses?" When Beezer offered that Napster had been designed "for fair use," Frackman took exception. "That may be what they tell you now," Frackman responded, but that was not Napster's intention. He quoted more from Parker: "It makes"—and they brag about this, Frackman said—"everyone a public server. They are integrally involved in the distribution to millions of people millions of recordings, the overwhelming number of which are copyrighted recordings owned by our clients." He pointed out that Parker—"the same person who is charged with Napster complying with the Digital Millennium Copyright Act"—himself downloaded plenty of copyrighted songs. The reasoning behind the "substantial noninfringing use" argument was absurd. "You say 'well, we may be able to get consent in the future from some people and therefore that permits us now to infringe almost everyone's copyright.' That's not what substantial non-infringing use could possibly mean! . . . They say maybe this could be used for the human genome project sometime in the future, so . . . I can now create and implement and supervise a system that now infringes copyrights billions at a time? It doesn't make any sense . . . . They say we're trying to narrow [the] Sony [case] but, your honor, they are trying to expand it way, way beyond the scope of Sony, way beyond the reasonableness of Sony."

The judges seemed very interested that no cases were "being pursued with U.S. attorneys." Because there was a criminal statute on the books, Beezer said he assumed that "with no expense to the record companies, I take it the government will file an indictment," as long as there was sufficient factual evidence of infringement. Frackman's answer was that the association and its members were not so interested in pursuing individuals. "There are millions of individuals out there . . . . We don't want to put an individual in jail for using the Napster system, we want to go to the source of the problem." Beezer's riposte that "a little public education through a criminal indictment goes a long way" caused a few chuckles.

At the end of the hearing, both sides rushed into a pressroom that was filled to bursting with cameras, lights, and reporters. The underdog Napster seemed to win most reporter sentiment, and, when Hilary Rosen stepped up, she was hit with plenty of aggressive questions. One reporter suggested that by going after Napster, the labels were really going to war with their consumers. Rosen agreed that it was very tricky territory: "It's very important what the record industry says to the users of Napster over the next four or five months. We have historically been very tolerant of downloaders but very aggressive of uploaders." She said that the RIAA, and its members, "care as much about the delivery of new music as anybody else," but, switching the focus away from labels back to artists, she said that they had "investments in these systems, in this creativity." Artists had an investment and the labels wanted to make sure that any compromise was not just a "one time feel-good solution. They're in this for the long haul, these systems have to work for the long haul, these services have to last over time, business models have to make sense, and there has to be a way for the music community to have these technologies work with them."

She said that the issue wasn't about eliminating users from sharing intellectual property as much as "does a business get to build several billion dollars' worth of assets on the backs of the creative community?" But what about Napster's hopes of working with the labels? "It's awfully difficult," Rosen explained, "to just spend forty minutes where Mr. Boies is arguing that they don't have to pay to hear them complaining that they want to pay. It's a little difficult to say which side of the equation we should be listening to from Napster." But she did hang something tantalizing out there, left unpursued. "There have been discussions with individual record companies and Napster," she said. "I can confirm that."

Fanning's life was getting very busy. Just a few days later, on October 9, Senator Hatch presided over an out-of-Washington congressional hearing at Bringham Young University, the perfect spot to highlight how hip he was to defend the ways young people got their music. The event was packed, though not because of Hatch, but because the leading figure of teenage rebellion, Shawn Fanning, was scheduled to speak. By having been kept almost totally silent and isolated by his company's PR and legal teams, Fanning had become a blank slate, easy to project onto. While Lars Ulrich also appeared before Congress, and traded memorabilia, his persona didn't click with as many people. Fanning was seen as much more compelling—these were times for boy wonders on their way to reaping millions, not necessarily rock stars bristling at defending theirs.

When it was Fanning's turn to speak, Hatch called those in the crowd who couldn't find seats to gather round him on the floor. He introduced Fanning with gushing praises that spilled over the top several times. "We're real proud of him, and the efforts he's made," while making Fanning more sympathetic by pointing out that "at nineteen years old, he still gets nervous." Hatch talked about how many, including Intel's Andy Grove, believed that P2P represented the future of the Internet. Fanning had been on more magazine covers than anyone since John F. Kennedy, Hatch said, and he added that, although he hoped that Fanning would keep doing what he was doing, "knowing a little about him, I think maybe he should run for office." This from one of the chief architects of the Digital Millennium Copyright Act. Fanning beamed at the support, a big smile on his face and a Brigham Young University baseball cap on top of his head. Hatch had a new, perhaps soon-to-be-rich, buddy.

Fanning delivered a speech that tread little new ground, going over why he built Napster and the inspiration for features like chatting. He did sound an increasingly urgent explanation that "Once there is collaboration, and not litigation, we can come to a peaceful conclusion and everything will work out." The lovefest ended as students crowded around a sunny, grinning Fanning, getting him to answer questions and sign autographs.

Fanning's smile just kept widening. On October 31, 2000, the first Halloween of the new millennium, the shocking news that one of the big five labels had made a deal with Napster seemed more apt for April Fool's day. But as the news rolled out, and a press conference was convened, it became clearer that this was no trick: Bertelsmann was partnering with Napster, and in a swift, bold move, the acquisition-hungry corporate leviathan had begun a deal that would bring a radical shift to its music division.

"I remember very well that I had some discussion with my colleagues in the industry a couple weeks ago," said Bertelsmann CEO Thomas Middelhoff, "and they said that if file sharing really has these continued growth rates, that in the future content would have no value. The great message of today is that we found a great way that content, that intellectual doing, that even with file-sharing will be an important part of the media entertainment industry. This is clearly the clear message for today." The CEO who had ruffled feathers in Germany a few weeks back by joking that the Frankfurt Bookfair, which had been going since the Renaissance, was now "the Bertelsmann book fair."

The relief of some kind of settlement seemed to have morphed into giddiness, as Middelhoff, the power behind the powerful BMG, was seen hugging Fanning, and Bertelsmann E-Commerce Group (BeCG) CEO Andreas Schmidt said in a press conference, "I'm really glad I met these guys." What was particularly telling was that the deal was announced under the auspices of Bertelsmann's e-commerce group, and not the music group. It clearly reflected both internal power shifts as well as what the company expected to be the future of the marketplace. Tellingly, there were no BMG executives present at the announcement.

For the preceding year BMG had been in the news mostly because its age policy had led to the dismissal of the flashy self-promoter and music industry legend, Clive Davis, who founded Arista records in 1975. Bertelsmann, which bought Arista in 1979, had a mandatory executive retirement policy at age 60. Davis, at 66, had long passed that mark, but remained a powerful force who did not go easily and raged hard with a PR campaign that led straight to the Grammys, at which he won honors for his work and was generally fawned over. Record producer Antonio "L.A." Reid replaced him in July as head of Arista, after a bitter six-month feud, and Davis went on to found J Records, ironically in partnership with BMG. Despite the ins and outs of industry prima donnas, the fact remained that BMG was not doing much to position itself for online music, not compared to the forces of Time Warner and AOL, and not enough to please Middelhoff, who saw the Internet as his way of making a mark.

The merger with AOL meant that Warner now had huge networks of consumers and a respected online veteran, Steve Case, behind the label. BMG's Web initiatives mostly followed the industry trends of investments and partnerships, with ARTISTdirect, Riffage.com, Egreetings Network, FanGlobe, Listen.com, and Eritmo.com. BMG was also developing a music site called Getmusic.com, to be operated jointly with Universal. The company made plans to sell tracks by artists like Clive

Davis's pals Whitney Houston and Santana, with songs at prices ranging from $1.98 to $3.49, and albums up to $16.98, via its own e-commerce sites and affiliates. The effort was named "Project Zeus." BMG was also publicly looking at the idea of a subscription model, but was reluctant to let anyone just walk away with its entire catalog for the price of one month. The usual disc-selling model remained the standard for the company, perhaps understandably when the income from that model was the highest it had ever been. It was BMG's parent company, Bertelsmann, that had been making most of the power deals. The company had a 44 percent stake in Lycos Europe as well as 40 percent of Barnes and Noble's BN.com. It bought CDNow in July 2000 for about $117 million, as well as the $42 million it took to pay off CDNow's debt and keep the business running. Middelhoff liked to compare the fledgling Napster to AOL when he first saw it in 1994 and convinced Bertelsmann to invest $50 million in the company (plus $100 million to launch AOL Europe). Both had similar grassroots growth, and both, he believed, stressed ease of use and networked community.

The terms of the deal, and more specifically, the expected workings of the new service, were vague, but included the confusing assurances from Hank Barry, Napster's CEO, that there would be no bothersome protection schemes, but instead an agreement that there would be security; a community model of sharing instead of pay-as-you-go; and affirmations by Boies in conferences and interviews that the building of the new service was in no way an admission of guilt that file sharing infringed copyrights. In fact, a statement by Bertelsmann's Schmidt that sales of CDs were not so affected by Napster use was additional ammunition for the court case. Bertelsmann agreed to withdraw from the copyright lawsuit, pending the development of the plan to its satisfaction. What Napster received from Bertelsmann was a loan to develop the technology to fulfill the vague outlines of a vision, as well as the stunning satisfaction of breaking, or, perhaps of joining, the cartel.

That night the two parties hit the town to toast their agreement. But Fanning was not as interested in celebration, as he was itching to get to work as soon as possible to build and implement the new service. Clearly, he was pining to put the bad-boy label behind him.

As far as Jim Griffin was concerned, the events of the day confirmed his predictions about where online media was going. While he didn't want to comment on the specifics of the deal, he believed in broad terms that "service is overtaking product, subscription winning over the product-based transaction."

Middelhoff suddenly appeared to have taken on some of the fame, and he quickly hit the media circuit. When he was on the Charlie Rose show, on public television, Rose teased the executive about having kept mum about the deal at a recent conference they'd both attended with many other industry leaders. "Why did you do it?" he asked. "Why did you break rank?" Middelhoff responded, "I thought, internally, 'what's going on here?' Napster had 38 million users, it has a tremendous growth rate, it's in some ways a phenomenon. What we have to do is not just fight them only in the court rooms—OK, we have to protect intellectual property rights—but we have to figure out what is the consumer really needing, and how can we give him the best service? And how can we deal, as a media and content industry, with the needs of our consumers as far as file sharing is concerned? So then I thought, it's really the appropriate time to sit together with the representatives of Napster, and try to figure out how we can find a bridge from their interests, the interests of our consumers, and our interests to protect intellectual property rights."

"File sharing in the future will be legitimate. My deep understanding, and my conviction is . . . that in the future file sharing is an important part of the value chain of the media and entertainment industry. Doesn't matter who will win in the courtroom. What I'm also seeing in the meantime is that the media and entertainment industries are trying to develop their own specific business models, but when I see the kind of brand awareness that Napster is having . . . . I think it's the best thing to integrate with them and not fight them. "

From his fellow industry executives, Middelhoff said that despite his worries, he "found more understanding and support than I had expected." Although the court case was still in full effect, minus one big participant, it felt as if the wall of denial that Ken Hertz compared to the war on drugs—complete distrust of the opposition—had eroded.

Still, Metallica's lawyer King made media appearances, vowing to fight on and expressing his conviction that Universal, just as in the MP3.com suit, would not drop the case.

Whatever the reactions by the other labels, the response from within the BMG record label was clearly bleak. The embrace of Napster was taken as a personal rebuke by the top brass, an explicit criticism of their inability to develop a working plan for the Internet—a vote of no confidence in their vision. The following Monday, Straus Zelnick, the president and CEO, and BMG founder Michael Dornemann announced their resignations. Middelhoff had, evidently, kept them unaware of the Napster deal until it was almost finished, and then hit them over the head with it, along with a massive corporate restructuring that would leave them with much less power. Middelhoff was reportedly upset with Zelnick over his handling of key label duties, such as the badly fumbled departure of Clive Davis, and fractious negotiations, including a lawsuit, with 'N Sync, one of the label's top money makers. The pair were set to be replaced by Rudi Gassner, a former BMG employee who had resigned that year following feuds with Zelnick and Dornemann.

For those who had watched online music fight an eight-year uphill battle against the industry, the news was not unexpected. Rob Lord, who was spending his time promoting Ralph Nader's campaign for president, didn't seem to think the deal was such a score, anyway. "BMG made the investment offer as a somewhat cynical entrée into the digital music world," he said. "The RIAA lawsuit pressured a fire sale and BMG was the first clever or duped company to pick the remnants." Perhaps because he had seen the inside workings of another rising media conglomerate, he seemed to think that the other companies might just as well build their own systems. "It will be very unlikely that the other major labels will join BMG's folly. Time Warner's got AOL's 25 million *paying* consumers already. Sony's got other plans. Universal wants blood."

If amends were being made, and personal scores being settled, Hilary Rosen evidently felt compelled to quell the animosity between Shawn Fanning and Lars Ulrich. She wrote a letter to Hank Barry, in which she explained that she hoped Fanning might try to make amends for the recent derision of the Metallica. "Indeed," she suggested, "You guys have fostered the abuse that Lars and the band have taken for standing up for their rights, rights which you have acknowledged in theory in the past but now have a financial interest in supporting since you are taking Bertelsmann's money." Rosen said that for taking a stand for artists, Metallica's members were her heroes, and that she was going to ensure that they would not be left out if everyone else benefited.

Aside from the interesting detail that the chief of the RIAA was now admitting that the file-sharing phenomenon, which had grown to millions of fans, might benefit all, the implied relationships within the letter raised a question: Now that Napster was a part of the machine, did this mean a better deal for everyone, or just another Internet pay day, this time for Fanning, Barry, and Hummer Winblad? Either way, those who made it through the storm were starting to enjoy the clearing weather. Lord, who stayed in close contact with Fanning—the two frequently chatted online—said that the Napster was finally feeling hopeful. "He's totally upbeat at the moment. You would be too if you saw a glimmer of light after being in a cave for months."

9

A PYRRHIC VICTORY?

S taring at a scrolling list of enticing song titles, ripped and free for
the plucking—music that would never appear in most, if any,
stores—it was easy to feel a deep melancholy for a musical under-
world that was at risk. Ian Clarke had said that the Internet was responsible for his personal development, and that of his generation;
the same was true for music. Even people who hadn't come of age
with Napster had quickly become thrilled with the arrangement, in
some cases reawakening their interest in music and transforming
themselves from passive to active listeners. It wasn't just free instant
access to big hits; it was that you could discover things that no radio
would play, uncover songs from years old memories. If online music
were shut down altogether there would be no more tracking down
the song your mother used to sing to you, no more *Fat Albert* theme
song, no more lost television live bootlegs from 1975, no more Jim
Morrison at a moment of unreleasable vulgarity jamming with Jimi
Hendrix. Napster itself was merely a vessel, but if the community of
music fans who filled it with their collections was being chased away,
each forced to retreat back to isolation, it would be a sad day. A new,

corporate-sanctioned model of Napster was no doubt on the way, but a romp through a controlled Disneyland never compared to the excitement of a wild Mardi Gras carnival. An approved version might make a lot of people money, but the raw connection, that exciting moment when my library was joined to yours, that was in danger. Was this progress or just rewards? There was certainly a lot of big talk on both sides.

The fact that over 50 million people had registered for Napster and so many used it daily fulfilled the forecasts of early Web prognosticators—one of our most fundamental cultural activities was on the brink of becoming fully networked, even with fierce opposition of the industry built to develop and exploit that culture. To take a far broader view, technology is developing that will enable all sorts of miraculous things; we'd better make up our minds whether legislating artificial scarcity is something we'd like to support.

I have no interest at all in making sure that others don't copy my collection of Led Zeppelin CDs. If anything I have an interest in them doing so, because if my disc is ever scratched I can make a duplicate of theirs. One might argue that the nature of ownership is different today. When giving something away, or even taking it, even if the original is unchanged, is branded "stealing," it flies in the face of common sense. On the other hand, a lack of reward for works of art and those who promote them would be damaging. Setting aside any snobbery or nostalgia, there's no question that the strong economic engine attached to music has deeply enriched our culture. Sure there's a lot of vulgarity, but there's also a lot more choice.

Few seriously think that musicians, or those who help them, shouldn't be rewarded for their work. The music industry wants people to grow up and embraces "education" as a way to get students to adopt a respectful attitude towards copyrights. But the industry had better show that it is prepared to mature, too. And not kill culture for the sake of profits, and to actually live up to all the hype it's been spouting about supporting "artists' rights." Particularly as the example of work-for-hire legislation (as well as most of the industry's history of artist contracts) portrays them in such a deeply negative light.

All bets were off until the RIAA case brought against Napster was resolved. Work on the new model that would result from the Bertelsmann/Napster partnership continued at a brisk pace, as Bertelsmann CEO Thomas Middelhoff, speaking to an international elite gathered at Davos, Switzerland, promised a working service by June or July of 2001. Napster CEO Hank Barry disputed the timetable, but agreed the work was continuing. Between the two of them, the price for a subscription to the new Napster was floated as somewhere between $4.99 and $15 a month.

Any reasonable assessment of the online future until the status of Napster itself was cleared up was virtually impossible. It was the 50-million-pound gorilla. A huge settlement and a clear-cut victory would have made big headlines and maybe given one side a self-righteous boost, but like most of life, the reality was more complex: a mixture of compromise, stubbornness, and progress—maybe not something to make the extremists on any side swoon, but a playing field that might be shared. For anything resembling the Napster as millions knew it, it looked serious but not hopeless.

On February 12, 2001, the three-judge panel from the Ninth Circuit Court of Appeals released its findings, which supported Patel's injunction and determined that Napster should be held liable for copyright infringement, despite a decision that the preliminary injunction was a little vague and needed some refining. The case was sent back to a lower court for resolution. A mortal blow to Napster? Not exactly, but certainly a grave one.

"The district court correctly recognized that a preliminary injunction against Napster's participation in copyright infringement is not only warranted but required," wrote Judge Beezer in the court's opinion. The court defined its duty as simply making sure that Patel got her law straight, and as far as they were concerned she had. "As long as the district court got the law right," said the court's ruling, "it will not be reversed simply because the appellate court would have arrived at a different result."

The Ninth Circuit judges obligingly cataloged many of the reasons why they felt Napster continued to infringe copyright, and the list was pretty damning. One by one the judges shot down most of Boies's arguments, as well as pleas for a court-brokered resolution that would allow the company to avoid paying massive damages. The three held that using Napster to "get something for free they would ordinarily have to buy" was a commercial use, and thus copyright infringement. "No evidence exists to support," they said, Napster's claims that the labels "implied" a license to their works by encouraging distribution of MP3 files. Napster "bears the burden of policing the system within the limits of the system."

Despite the list of abuses, the judges felt that the scope of Patel's injunction needed to be changed. The preliminary injunction, they said, was "overbroad because it places on Napster the entire burden of ensuring that no 'copying, downloading, uploading, transmitting, or distributing' of plaintiffs' works occur on the system." In order for Napster to be held accountable, the judges said, it had to (1) receive "reasonable knowledge of specific infringing files with copyrighted musical compositions and sound recordings; (2) know or should know that such files are available on the Napster system; and (3) fail to act to prevent viral distribution of the works . . . . The mere existence of the Napster system, absent actual notice and Napster's demonstrated failure to remove the offending material, is insufficient to impose contributory liability."

A request by Napster for a court-ordered royalty payment was roundly rejected. "Napster tells us that 'where great public injury would be worked by an injunction, the courts might . . . award damages or a continuing royalty instead of an injunction in such special circumstances.'" The judges were "at a total loss" to find any "special circumstances" simply because this case applied established doctrines of copyright law to a new technology. Worse, they were not at all buying the idea of "public injury." Imposing a compulsory royalty payment schedule would give Napster an "easy out" of this case, they said. "If such royalties were imposed, Napster would avoid penalties for any future violation of an injunction, statutory copyright damages and any possible criminal penalties for continuing infringement. The royalty structure would also grant Napster the luxury of either choosing to continue and pay royalties or shut down. On the other hand, the wronged parties would be forced to do business with a company that profits from the wrongful use of intellectual properties."

For most students the news was gloomy. Newspapers and Web sites across the country ran stories interviewing random students on campuses. Most agreed with eighteen-year-old Michael Sheen from UC Berkeley, quoted in the *San Francisco Chronicle* saying that he and most of his friends got their music predominantly from Napster. Others, like Ted Yoon, nineteen, offered some hope for those in the business of selling discs: "I guess I will go back to buying CDs," he said.

The ruling left Shawn Fanning and company, along with their German bodyguard, in a much weaker position to make deals with the other four biggies. On the other hand, the prospect of a fire sale might have given the labels a little more resolve to come to an agreement that would most likely be very favorable to them. The future for the RIAA was shaping up to be a lot more comfortable.

The association was, of course, very pleased. In a press conference, Hilary Rosen repeated the company line that Napster's business model was "built on infringement" and was not only morally and legally wrong, but was also "a threat to the development of the legitimate online music market." It was an odd statement because it is clear that the legitimate music market choices that she held up as advances would be nowhere nearly as innovative were it not for Napster's popularity. "The choices available to consumers of legitimately licensed music are now much, much greater than just a year ago. Music on the Internet based on a subscription model is around the corner," she said, ignoring that MP3.com and Emusic were already offering just that, largely out of desperate competition with Napster. It was also strange that she would pull out an appeal to nationalism, pointing out that 30 percent of Napster users were not Americans when 80 percent of the big five labels weren't American either. Regardless, Rosen painted the victory as one for nationalism: "American intellectual property is our nation's greatest trade asset. We cannot stand by idly as our rights and our nation's economic assets are in jeopardy or dismissed by those who would negate its value for their own enrichment." Of course, those who drove legislation to extend corporate ownership of copyrights, keeping them away from artists, for their own enrichment—as the RIAA tried in the work-for-hire scandal—were just fine. Rosen called on Napster to "stand down" and build its business "the old fashioned way . . . by seeking permission first."

While he might have been forgotten by Rosen, Emusic chairman Gene Hoffman was also happy about the ruling and was no doubt hoping that it would bring some hope for his troubled company. He called the decision a fair reaffirmation of the rights of copyright holders: "This should establish a clear foundation for the growth of legitimate music download services on the Internet—where artists, labels, and consumers all have a voice in how digital music is enjoyed." But would Emusic be around to enjoy such a world? That was unclear, and the company was looking for any good news it could find, because it certainly wasn't attracting many big bands or large downloads. A look at the Emusic charts at the beginning of 2001 showed that the long-running They Might Be Giants was still the top-selling band. Frank Black was still in the top ten. It's not at all a snub of either of those acts to speculate that such an ossified chart was a sign of a serious lack of movement at Emusic. The company was undergoing financial strains, laid off employees and even pulled the plug on the Internet Underground Music Archive, or IUMA. On February 7, five days before the Napster ruling, IUMA cofounder Jeff Patterson, who was still working there, sent out a letter to artists stating that the company would basically suspend operations, while seeking a backer. But finding a buyer or backer when "Web site" had become synonymous with failure proved to be impossible. No one even wanted to bankroll a legend. "As the Internet revolutionizes the way music is distributed, independent artists have gained unprecedented access to fans throughout the world," Patterson wrote. "Unfortunately, it hasn't come without costs. This has been a hard time for Internet music companies as the rules that govern what we do change on a daily basis. Many of our competitors and peers are either going out of business or dealing with myriads of lawsuits waged against them. No one seems to be making it through this tough time unscathed, IUMA included."

Napster CEO Hank Barry issued a sad response that he was disappointed with the court for dealing such a heavy strike against Napster before a full trial could happen. "The Napster community is about the love of music. Napster community members love music and purchase far more CDs than most people. They share files with no expectation of gain. We have again and again stated that we intend to make payments to artists, songwriters and other rightsholders. Yet the largest and most successful media companies in the world have taken aim at our more than 50 million users, and today they have landed a blow. We will respond and deal with this situation in the courts."

Manufacturers of electronics devices, who never seemed to have trouble getting paid, were not pleased with any prospect of a slowdown in consumer adoption of the MP3 format. Gary Shapiro, the president of the Consumer Electronics Association, was quick to denounce the ruling, pointing out that the Ninth Circuit was the same court that ruled that the VCR was illegal before the ruling was overturned by the Supreme Court. "If that decision had stood, we would have no VCR or movie rentals—to the detriment of Hollywood and American consumers. We can only wonder if this ruling stands how technology and consumer access will be limited in the future." Shapiro warned that if "the content industry has its way, the 'play' button will become the 'pay' button, widening the digital divide and stalling the revolution in instant, global access to education, information and entertainment."

Senator Orrin Hatch also took exception to the circuit court's ruling, and what his comments lacked in commitment, they made up for in length and volume. It was either ironic or appropriate, because Hatch was one of the crafters of the Digital Millennium Copyright Act that was referred to eight times in the ruling. In a statement before the Senate, Hatch said that the Judiciary Committee would need to hold hearings "on the decision's possible implications and to get an update on developments in the online music market." He was worried that shutting down Napster might deprive "more than 50 million consumers access to a music service they have enjoyed." While he affirmed that he was a strong believer in copyright and an artist's right to compensation, and admitted "Napster as it currently operates, threatens this principle," he understood that copyright had survived alongside "society's evolving technologies" for generations. Technology works to make a bigger pie for everyone, he believed, and if fully baked, Napster could make one hell of a pie. "It is, quite simply, a virtual community of unprecedented reach and scale. It is the most popular application in the history of the Internet."

While admitting that in the same position he'd probably do as the labels did, by seeking relief under laws that he'd helped write, Hatch was worried that the battle might escalate to the point where "the erosion of the copyright laws might be the frightening outcome." If Napster were shut down, consumers might flock to Gnutella or Freenet, which would undermine copyright on the Net, as well as artists' rights. He said he felt the gnawing concern that "legal victory for the record labels may prove Pyrrhic or short-sighted." Working together in the marketplace cooperatively will lead to the best result for all parties, the record labels, the online music services, the artists, and the music fans. Hatch said he hoped the focus would be on the latter two. "After all, without artists, there is nothing to convey, and without the fans, there is no one to convey it to. I think keeping the focus on the artists and the audience can help the technologists and the copyright industries find a way for all to flourish. And I hope this opportunity is taken before it is lost."

If Hatch was concerned with the outcome of Napster on legal grounds, he also had a personal interest: Manus Cooney, who had been Hatch's chief policy and political adviser in his role as counsel for the Senate Judiciary Committee, had been hired in early December to be Napster's vice president for corporate and policy development. Napster was continuing its efforts to get some of the biggest guns on it side. Though it didn't have anywhere near the resources of the RIAA, bright stars like Boies and Cooney—along with an incredibly large user base— were the main things going for the firm.

As Hilary Rosen grappled with concern about foreigners draining America of its intellectual property, in Europe, it appeared her RIAA predecessor was hard at work putting an end to the practice. The International Federation of the Phonographic Industry, which was led by former RIAA chairman Jay Berman, seemed to be behind Belgian police raids of file traders' homes. According to an Associated Press report, there were three raids in December and January, prompted by warnings from Belgian IFPI chief Marcel Heymans, who boasted that he was using software to track online traders. The Belgian police spokesman said that there were seven cases under review, over half of which were Napster users. Efforts to prosecute the file traders had been suggested by Ninth Circuit Judge Beezer in the appeals hearing, but RIAA lawyer Frackman had demurred. Perhaps Belgium was to be a testing ground for this technique, to see if it would cause too much outcry, or work to curb trading.

Shawn Fanning, though, was focused on making a new version of Napster that wouldn't spur a police action. Instead of commenting directly on the case or judgment, Fanning stayed in character, keeping his role as earnest hard worker: "We've been developing a Napster service that offers additional benefits to members of the community and, importantly, makes payments to artists. I'm focused on building this better service and I still hope to have it in place this year. The new technologies we are developing are amazing; I hope that, by further court review or by agreement with the record companies, we can find a way to share them with the community." Fanning was always someone with whom the labels could negotiate, because he was never fueled by the ideological passions that drove someone like Ian Clarke. It was interesting that Fanning would become a hero to the traders, rather than an ideologue like Clarke or Gene Kan. While Fanning created the program that became a success, he seemed to have done it just because he could, stumbling into it as much as anything.

He certainly had his work cut out for him. Despite the harsh realities of a big lawsuit and dwindling investment, few wanted to come out and predict the death of Napster, especially on the record. One longtime insider did predict that no matter what happened with Bertelsmann, Napster would soon be eclipsed: "I doubt that Napster will be a brand, product, or service a year from now," said the insider, who asked not to be identified, right after the Bertelsmann deal was announced. "Net brand name half-lives are very short. Music sub-scription services will be available from all your favorite oligarchy-approved portals. Napster's ability to convert pirates to consumers will be a slow, hard sell. And Gnutella, Freenet and other pirate tools will offer plunderings beyond Fanning's fantasies."

The workings of the new Napster were a little vague, but the company was aiming for a service that would offer labels a chance to opt in and would provide them with a huge money-making opportunity. The files traded would be restricted by a protection scheme of some sort, one that was likely to keep fans from making CDs from downloaded songs. Napster and Bertelsmann were determined to retain the peer-to-peer architecture, which kept the experience exciting and familiar for current users and kept the overhead low. How songs would be tracked and artists and copyright holders paid was the subject of hard work and intense negotiation. But not all labels were moving along into the Napster settlement as quickly as the company would like, particularly when they had the court victory to mull (and possibly gloat) over. AOL wanted to build its own trading network, and certainly had more resources than Bertelsmann; Vivendi Universal seemed to be following its premerger ways, as Jean-Marie Messier said that he would wait until the legal outcome was determined before he'd settle. He'd probably get a better deal and a legal settlement as well.

But the fact that these companies were talking seriously about faults with their online systems meant that progress was well under way. Andreas Schmidt, the CEO of Bertelsmann's newly created online umbrella, the E-Commerce Group, told CNET that any system offered by the majors, "whether it's from Universal, whether it's from BMG, whether it's from Warner Music, doesn't help the customer right now to get what he wants and what he deserves . . . easy, simple access to music." No matter if the download tools were from Universal's Bluematter, Sony, or BMG, the outcome was the same: their computer crashes. "It's a complete mess-up in terms of technology; it's a complete mess-up in terms of ease of use. I think we have to do something about it," Schmidt said. But on the bright side, he said that there was no longer a "holy war" against Napster and that all sides were at least open to a serious discussion about the service; the only hard part was hammering out all the details.

"The thing that scares providers of intellectual property is that the digital delivery in some ways takes them out of the supply equation," industry guru Jim Griffin had said a few months earlier. "They no longer control the quantity or the destiny of their product." Griffin warned that major labels were in fact major distributors, working hard to protect their manufacturing and distribution infrastructure that had been built with sweat and guts. But as companies like AOL Time Warner and Bertelsmann became more enthusiastic about their data infrastructure and customer base, it was clear they wouldn't sacrifice the bits for the bricks. The heavy hand of copyright wasn't going to wither and be tossed aside along with society's mental shackles, but the fact of life that millions of Napster users were probably not going away surely gave the RIAA pause. Any company that failed to take advantage of such a large, energized group wouldn't be worth its salt. There was a revolution in play, as Bertelsmann began restructuring and taking on some top heads that gave away a little about the game Middelhoff intended to play.

The excitement of online rebellion may have had some wind knocked out of it, but there was no denying that the pipeline that consumers used to get their music had changed. All realistic projections of how music would be distributed going forward had been altered. And from the consumer's point of view as well as most musicians', the change would be for the better. No matter what happened to Napster, online music was set to break a stranglehold over distribution and airplay.

Certainly Gnutella's Gene Kan, Freenet's Clarke, and others were waiting in the wings to take over if Fanning stumbled, but no one ever thought that Napster was anything more than the sum of its users. Just as a fax machine would not be so useful if only one other person had one, a file-trading program without a backdrop of diverse users would quickly become useless.

A few days after the Ninth Circuit ruling, there was a P2P conference in San Francisco sponsored by O'Reilly, a publisher of software guides that had become a respected player in the open-source movement. Of course, the Napster decision dominated most of the dialogue. While music was important to them, most of the voices expressed concern with precedents that might kill the developing peer-to-peer model or trample online privacy. With figures such as Fanning, Clarke, and Gene Kan in attendance, John Perry Barlow railed against the courts and encouraged listeners to focus their efforts on resisting the law. "After (Monday's) Ninth Circuit case, I think the only way to deal with law on the Internet is to ignore it flagrantly," he said. "I want everyone in this room to consider themselves revolutionaries and go out and develop whatever they damn well please, whatever the law says."

Stanford Professor Lawrence Lessig, who was not nearly as given to radical pronouncements as Barlow, was fired up as well. Lessig had complained about an innovation-killing environment that was being created when copyright industries worked so hard against initiatives like My MP3.com. He called Robertson's effort a pretty creative attempt to add value to a music purchase for the consumer and praised it for taking steps to keep people from misusing the system. Still the industry killed it, and the legal system's response was to say "we're going to punish you as strongly as we can." That was going to seriously hurt innovation, especially in regards to P2P. "In a free society one would think we're not worried about that, but the point is this is anathema to the interests of the copyright industry."

In the conference's keynote address, Lessig wondered whether the rush to litigation would stifle progress, especially by those without the resources of MP3.com or Napster. "I thought we knew the Internet was going to mess things up, that it was going to change things, and we the lawyers were going to commit ourselves to watching and waiting," Lessig said. The professor explained that in cases like *Reno v. ACLU*, which had to do with online pornography, the Supreme Court decided that the Internet was developing and would be very important, so it made sense to wait and see what happened rather than rushing to legislate. But with the vast wealth and lobbying resources, the entertainment industry was busy making sure that would no longer apply. "To the extent the legal system perceives this new technology as focused on one particular application, then the development of this new architecture will be hampered by that one application's legal baggage. But it is as silly to think about P2P as applying just to music as it would have been to think about the Internet as applying just to pornography. Whatever the initial use of the technology, it has nothing to do with the potential of the architecture to serve many other extremely important functions."

Those lobbying resources—vast as they might be—were in the process of being upgraded. While Fanning had a friend in Orrin Hatch, the RIAA was working around the clock to shed its image as a Democrats-only club, building up connections within the Republican power structure. The first up was Bob Dole, former Senate majority leader and war hero, in his capacity as lobbyist. Evidently it was up to "the greatest generation" to pitch in and preserve the musical rights of Metallica, Eminem, and Dr. Dre. This was an interesting role for someone who had, a few years earlier, vehemently denounced the industry, and especially its rap acts, for encouraging the nation's "moral degradation."

Which companies will come out on top because of online music? Clearly the record companies seem to have the short-term advantage. Napster use never seemed to slow their business, they've made a good amount from MP3.com settlements alone, and a future file-trading network that cuts them in should provide a windfall. Even better off are their parent companies, which have tried to position themselves away from the old dependence on pressing plants and trucks. AOL, Vivendi, Bertelsmann: they all will do very well under a Net-centric future. Sony in particular could profit if it makes relevant devices that spark consumer imagination, but so far it has shown very little vision in crafting products to work with online music.

Despite the efforts of Microsoft to usurp its position, RealNetworks continued to dominate the world of streaming and made considerable headway in delivered music as well. The company's smart software and market leadership kept it on top. Liquid gets credit for vision, even if it was painful to see that it had not reaped the benefits that founder Gerry Kearby had hoped for. The company did so many things right, and so many things first that it seemed to be a shoe-in for market leader. But an unfriendly distribution scheme and the irresistible convergence of the MP3 format and P2P took the wind out of Liquid Audio's sails, despite plenty of money and a very friendly position with artists, labels, and retailers. It was questionable whether even dramatic court victories of the RIAA against Napster would help Liquid Audio recover. There were rumors that surfaced in November that Bertelsmann was considering a takeover of the company. Perhaps a new, more policed Internet would be more fertile ground.

Whether it was sneaky or just plain smart, a company called Gracenote built a user-generated database of all the CDs that MP3 users ripped, therefore becoming a ubiquitous component of nearly every online player, and the company planned to leverage that wealth into a bright future—one that could work no matter who gained the upper hand in the Napster wars. Gracenote's president, David Hyman, an American who in an earlier incarnation sold stereos out of his van as he traveled across Europe, left a powerful post at Sonicnet and MTV's interactive portal to head a company that was getting over 18 million "calls" to its database a month, about 40 percent of them from outside the United States. While that number wasn't quite on the level of Napster, it was an impressive number that was organized and constantly feeding something that no one else had: the ability to distinguish virtually every CD ever made, including song titles, band name, and genre. Because most of those calls were made as users ripped CDs, and the information was encoded along with the CD, Gracenote had a method of telling what users were playing. What was especially intriguing was that Hyman intended to harness this ability to build a platform for content, commerce, and services to fit with online listening. "Once you can recognize what the consumer is listening to, you can provide them with advertising-supported content, e-commerce opportunities, you can provide them with other service opportunities like ticket sales," Hyman said. "It fundamentally changes the music-listening experience."

Gracenote was building a "music browser" similar, Hyman said, to RealJukebox, which they would license to whomever wanted it.

Efforts like that, whether made by Gracenote or Bertelsmann, would be a good way to generate revenue while adding to the consumer experience. Because his model would work best when more people were trading and listening, Hyman was free to support whatever consumers wanted. "I'm a firm believer that whenever you make music more accessible to consumers, the whole market goes up. Yeah, there's going to be more pirating but in the aggregate they're going to make more money."

For many of those who were interested in music for its own sake, like Rob Lord, the online music revolution has had a deep effect. For Lord it was simply an outgrowth of who he was. "I was basically trying to uproot my record store experience and make it so that no one would ever have to sell a bad pop record again. There was a definite sense that if people had access to more and better things . . . this would accelerate that process, and put people in touch with things that were more meaningful to them, that were more meaningful to the audience; create a better world essentially . . . . Despite the fact that Napster rips the economics out of things, people are getting to hear much more, and are deciding much more for themselves and their groups of friends. Look at the evolution of so many sub-genres. That's due in large part to the Internet."

Other music fans, even those involved in music on the Net, had deep reservations about it. "I hate digital music," said Frederic Madre, a French editor of European music portal Vitaminic. "It's like listening to the radio except you don't discover anything 'cause you're the DJ. The CD dragged music out of the culture area into the industry of entertainment simply by inventing a format that made it easier to use than the vinyl, adding features that have nothing to do with music (display of track time, shuffling, etc.) and everything to do with pushing new hardware on you. MP3 is taking this even further: without a box or a sleeve left to explain the relation of the artists to the world they live in, music is stripped of all its potential to transform your life."

At least it was free. But would it continue to be free? Yes, there's no question that music will be free in some form always. Once music hits the air, anyone is able to record it. Even a RIAA-supported police clampdown on file trading would leave room for determined souls to trade. Would creativity suffer if music were to be forever free? There's no question that economics has driven the industry and is responsible like nothing else for the unbelievable selection of music that the consumer has had up until now. Despite what you might imagine from the companies' hysteria, a great deal of amateur piracy is a built-in cost of the industry and has been since the cassette tape. But unless Freenet becomes as ubiquitous and easy to use as Napster, it might hit an ironic reversal of Jim Griffin's exhortation to "feel free," a service that is free but doesn't feel free because it is so hard to use. On the other hand, a digital "celestial jukebox" that felt free because users weren't always thinking about how much they paid still sounds remarkably compelling if someone can pull it off. If it could fairly reward artists at all levels, then few, except perhaps grumpy cultural critics, could find fault with it.

There is a positive sign that all the big five record companies might actually work something out: there is a shift away from the old music industry days documented in *Hit Men* when all bosses hated each other. Bertelsmann's Thomas Middelhoff, AOL's Steve Case, and Jean-Marie Messier of Vivendi are friends with much in common (and are even reported to share messages with each other throughout the day using AOL buddy lists). Though AOL Time Warner's CEO Gerald Levin was reported as saying that "music companies don't play well together," these executives are more accustomed to working in the merger-crazy corporate environment in which lines between companies are a lot fuzzier than in the past. The management at AOL Time Warner and BMG also had some movement between them, but it was hard to say whether it was a sign of reconciliation or aggressive hiring. After Bertelsmann moved ahead with its Napster deal against the wishes of most of its music group execs, BMG underwent a shake-up in which many left, such as its president of new media, Kevin Conroy. AOL abruptly hired Conroy to lead its AOL Music Unit, the new umbrella for online music, including Winamp and Spinner. And while AOL was picking up ex-BMG honchos, Bertelsmann shocked the world—and revealed a little about its ambitions—by picking Joel

Klein, the former assistant attorney general who led the Microsoft antitrust suit, as its U.S. chairman and CEO. The move was clear: Bertelsmann wanted to expand, control the distribution, and avoid any antitrust problems that might bring. At the same time, Klein might help to keep AOL, which still had the much bigger network and expertise, in check.

As the corporate world buzzes with mergers and suits, and technologists build new systems, have artists themselves gained anything by the rise of online music? The Web has only been a serious social force for half a decade, and it's only now that fast connections are starting to be popularly available. It's only natural that most of its effects, most of its new ideas have yet to germinate. Yet it's clear that the availability of online music has spurred new outlets, many very surprising. Online newspapers, another force that has yet to fully realize its potential, have begun to offer services that promote and distribute local music. In late January 2001, the Washingtonpost.com launched its hub for the capitol's MP3 scene. Others, like the *Boston Globe's* Boston.com, have also had interesting success, attracting young audiences to newspapers and attempting to move a little into the hip entertainment space controlled by weekly free papers.

The development of many different channels for music serving diverse communities—most ignored by the traditional industry—could bring with it the ability for greater numbers of musicians to make a decent living selling fewer records than the 100,000 or so needed to break even on a major label. It was that hope that drove Ice-T to start his own online label. He expressed a "loss of enthusiasm with traditional record labels and how much money it takes to really be a player in that game. Because you usually don't have the money so you have to end up dealing with people who may not be on the same artistic level as you, or who don't see things the way you see them. And finally, the music I like isn't traditional pop music, it's more underground stuff, so I wanted to put myself in a position where my artists could sell three or four thousand records and still see a check."

The excitement over P2P might have been fueled by Napster, but it was certainly picked up by some of computing's biggest powers. Intel became quickly enamored of the concept, and like others who worried about being the last on the next Web train, made sure it had its bags packed. While giving credit to Napster, Gnutella, and Freenet as the "spark" for peer-to-peer computing, Intel CEO Patrick Gelsinger described in a speech at his company's developers' forum a "vision of a billion connected computers, connecting everything, every PC, every other device, building this massive fabric. And we are marching very well on our way toward the billion connected computers." Intel's "agenda" he said, was that P2P "is the revolution that could change computing as we know it." Of course Intel would profit if a need for greater processing power sold more chips. But the return to the excitement that drove the building of the Net was dramatic, concrete, and an interesting goal when so much of the frenzy over building Net business had met a swing against it. Gelsinger described the moment as one of revelation: With the dramatic amount of infrastructure that's had been built, a new perspective on that computing infrastructure had been revealed. "Napster, Gnutella, FreeNet are the spark which shows the picture which emerges. And we suggest that it could be ushering in this next computer revolution."

Online music, sprung from the Internet infrastructure built by visionaries like Tim Berners-Lee, had helped the Net evolve in the direction its makers imagined. Aside from the service of e-mail, MP3 trading was the first large-scale benefit of using computers to connect everyone. How to accomplish that fairly was one of the first major hurdles to dealing with a networked future that would benefit all. The baggage of the recording industry, from greedy bullying to legitimate gripes and years of experience, was met head-on with the stridency of online advocates and the enthusiasm of music lovers. With a massive fabric of a billion connected computers, some rules were necessary; who would set them, and how, was the problem.

Despite the RIAA's legal victories, it was clear, from the structure of who controlled the companies and their visions of the future, that the Napster community—its users—was about to score the biggest win. Of course it wasn't a zero-sum game: a win for consumers might still mean billions in industry profits. If the law came down too restrictively it wouldn't be a zero-sum loss, either.

Outside any cycles of hype and stock market ups and downs, the scope and accelerating power of the personal computer when combined with the Internet make it an advance for exchanging information unlike any other. Is it any surprise that a development of that magnitude might have repercussions for businesses? If the entertainment industry is not able to deal with the ubiquity and free flow of information in the information age then it will suffer. If it takes a knee-jerk reactionary role and gets short-sighted laws passed, then we'll all suffer. There's a chance that the industry will live up to its own words and craft a solution that pays artists fairly, is not overly restrictive of fair use, and leaves the market open for broad tastes. If it can accomplish that, then it will have begun to make up for a century of screwing its artists. The money it will earn back should smooth any ruffled feathers over a couple years of free trading.

NOTES

Chapter 1

p. 15   **In 1993 . . .** *Information Technology Research and Development: Information Technology for the 21st Century*, White House Office of the Press Secretary, January 21, 2000

p. 16   **"The Web," . . .** http://www.w3.org/1998/02/Potential.html

p. 17   **"The actual explosion . . ."** http://www.w3.org/People/Berners-Lee/UU.html

p. 20   **If our property . . .** "The Economy of Ideas," *Wired*, March 1994

Chapter 3

pp. 46–47   **"Well, you know . . ."** Fool.com, May 23, 2000 "Fool Interview with Michael Robertson"

p. 51   **"drives a Mercedes . . ."** *Los Angeles Times*, September 13, 2000, "Latin Grammy Fund-Raising Puts Spotlight on Academy," Chuck Philips

p. 53   **"Some of my . . ."** *San Diego Metro*, February, 1999, "The E-Music Man"

Chapter 4

p. 68   **"The demand for . . ."** SonicNet.com; November 10, 1998

Chapter 5

p. 81–82   **In the famously . . .** *Hit Men*, Fredric Dannen, 1991

p. 87   **"The scrutiny is . . ."** "A Chat with Hilary Rosen," *Wired News*. October 2, 2000.

p. 88   **"How do we . . ."** *Wired News*, same story.

Chapter 6

p. 102　　　　**"One of the richest . . ."** *Business Week*, April 12, 2000

p. 102　　　　The wealth guitarist . . . *Business Week*

p. 104　　　　**"I've always thought . . ."** *Business Week*

p. 105　　　　**"We are big . . ."** CBS Market Watch

p. 106　　　　**"There's no difference . . ."** *Toronto Sun*, May 12, 1999

pp. 111–112　**"Good Riddance . . ."** "Good Riddance to Napster.com," *IDS News*, February 16, 2000

p. 112　　　　**In February 2000 . . .** "Save Our Napster, Say Students," *Wired News*, February 17, 2000

p. 112　　　　**Fundamentally I think . . .** "Copyright Defendant Napster on Other Side in Dispute," CNET News.com, January 26, 2000

p. 113　　　　**They're perjuring . . .** "Napster Fans to Metallica: Prove It," *Salon*, May 16, 2000

p. 116　　　　**Middelhoff called . . .** "BMG Downloads Coming Next Month," *Consumer Electronics*, August 28, 2000

p. 124　　　　**He told *Salon* . . .** "Napster at Law," *Salon*, May 30, 2000

Chapter 7

p. 141　　　　**"Here you have . . ."** "David Boies: The Wired Interview," by John Heilemann, *Wired*, October 2000

p. 146　　　　**In July, AOL . . .** "AOL and InterTrust: A Legal Napster," *The Industry Standard*, July 10, 2000

pp. 147–148　**In an online diary . . .** http://www.webdog.org/

pp. 152–153　**The RIAA represents . . .** http://www.disciplineglobalmobile.com/diary/diary-RobertFripp.shtml

Chapter 8

p. 156　　　　**"That rubbed me . . ."** "Digital Music's Nasty Little War." *Wired News*, October 10, 2000

p. 167　　　　**Whatever the reactions . . .** "BMG Entertainment executives leaving," *Los Angeles Times*. November 5, 2000

Chapter 9

pp. 178–179　**"It's a complete . . ."** "Bertelsmann: Making music with Napster," Jim Hu, CNET. http://news.cnet.com/news/0–1005–201–4735496–0.html

p. 180　　　　**In the conference's . . .** "Lessig: Fight for Your Right to Innovate," David Sims, http://www.openp2p.com/pub/a/p2p/2001/02/16/lessig.html

p. 181　　　　**"To the extent . . ."** "Code + Law: An Interview with Lawrence Lessig," Tim O'Reilly and Richard Koman. http://openp2p.com/pub/a/p2p/2001/01/30/ lessig.html

INDEX

Advertising
  revenue from, 54, 56
Aerosmith, 28
Albini, Steve, 127
Albums, 109
  development of, 69
A&M Records, 82
Amazon.com, 40
Ampex, 41
Andreesson, Marc, 97
Angry Coffee, 134
AOL, 109
  Gnutella and, 146–148
  InterTrust and, 146–147
  Winamp/Nullsoft in, 97–98, 132,
    147–149
AOL Music Group, 184
AOL Time Warner, 82–83, 164, 178
  AOL purchase of Time Warner and,
    84, 109, 145
  customers *vs.* purchasers of, 179
  other labels and, 184–185
  record companies and holdings of,
    84
  setting up for Net-centric future by,
    181
Apple Computer
  Super Bowl ad by, 63
Ariola Records, 82
Arista Records, 82, 164
Artist Direct, 56, 95, 149, 164
  IPO of, 123

Artists. *See also* Musicians
  blanket licensing agreement and, 122
  famous through sharing of music by, 8
  Garageband.com and unknown, 73
  Internet promotion of interests of,
    65–66
  investment by, 162
  IUMA and unknown, 14–16, 51
  MP3.com payment to, 144–145
  MP3.com settlement and, 122
  name, music as valuable property of,
    77
  name recognition of, 89, 128–129
  need for listeners by, 61
  as partners, 95
  as rebel, 8
  record companies, renegotiation of
    contract and, 151
  against record company, 52, 59,
    126–127
  Riffage and unknown, 94–95
  rights of, 54–55, 170, 176
  respect for, 10
  self-marketing on Net by, 44
  technology freeing of, 63
  work-for-hire, 126, 170, 174
Artists Against Piracy, 125
ASCAP (American Society of
    Composers, Authors and
    Publishers), 24–25
Atlantic Records, 24, 84, 133
Audience. *See* Fans

Audio compression, 13, 38–39
Audio Home Recording Act of 1992,
    57, 58, 141
Audio streaming, 39–40, 42
Audiocassette, 3

Badfinger, 68
The Band, 68
Bandwidth
    faster, 40
    slower, 35, 38
Barlow, John Perry, 19–21, 38, 180
Barry, Hank, 124, 140, 157, 165,
    167–168, 175
Beam-It, 119–122
Beastie Boys, 30, 56
    Artist Direct and, 123
    live recordings on Web site by, 66–67
    Website of, 65–66
Beatles, 74, 83
Beck, 108, 123
Berman, Jay, 177
Bernstein, Keith, 124–125
Bertelsmann, 116
    AOL and, 109
    AOL Europe and, 165
    CDNow purchased by, 109, 165
    customers vs. purchasers of, 179
    holdings under, 82–83, 165
    Liquid Audio and, 182
    Napster changes and, 178
    Napster, growth of sales of and, 165
    Napster purchased by, 163–165, 167,
        171, 184
    other labels and, 184–185
    setting up for Net-centric future by,
        181
    withdraw of copyright Napster
        lawsuit by, 165
Bertelsmann Music Group (BMG), 1,
    13, 5, 23, 96, 110. See also BMG
    Music Service
    Bertelsmann E-Commerce Group
        (BeCG) and, 164, 178
    executives resign after Napster from,
        167

Getmusic.com by, 164
InterTrust and, 146
'N Sync vs., 167
online involvement by, 96, 164–165
Project Zeus by, 165
record companies and holdings
    under, 82–83
Besonic.com, 73
Best Buy, 76
Big Black, 126
Billboard, 14
Black, Frank, 93, 174
Blanket licensing agreement, 122
BMG Music Service, 82–83
BMI (Broadcast Music Incorporated), 5,
    24
Boies, David, 140–141, 157–158, 162,
    165
Boston.com, 185
Bowie, David, 26, 64–65
BowieNet, 65
Brand, Stewart, 18
Bringman, Hal, 49, 50, 53, 58, 72, 77
Bronfman, Edgar Jr., 24, 138–140
Brooks, Garth, 83
Bruce, Dunstan, 4
Bugzilla, 134
Bulletin board system (BBS), 17
Burger, James, 58–59
Burly Bear cable network, 94
The Byrds, 64

Cactus Data Shield technology, 110
Canal+, 82
Capitol Records, 83
    Internet as marketing tool by, 66
    Internet live recordings and, 67
    Liquid Audio and, 45–46
Case, Steve, 184
The Cavern Club, ix-xiii
CBS Records, 82, 83, 164
CDs
    anachronistic value of, 34
    burner, 110
    Cactus Data Shield technology for,
        110

copyright violation on individual, 143
development of, 6
enhanced, 26, 27
Gracenote and database of, 182
instability of, 109
Napster and growth of sales of, 152, 165
non-watermarking of, 62, 109–110
online, 109
ripper, 96
watermarks and, 93
CDNOw, 165
CD-ROM, 26, 90
interactive, 68
Center for Computer Research in Music and Acoustics, 42
Chat rooms, 71
Cher, 123
Chess records, 63
Chiariglione, Leonardo, 91, 109
Chrysalis Records, 83
Chuck D, 10, 64–65, 125, 128
Chumbawamba, 4
Clarke, Ian, 134–139, 169, 177, 179–180
Cleans, 126
Clinton, Bill, 11–12
CNET, 36, 39, 112, 178
news.com, 98
Codec, 27
Cohen, Ted, 25–26, 27, 82, 116, 149–150
Amazon.com and, 151
EMI and, 149–152
College campus. *See also* Universities
downloading of music on, 2–3, 47, 109, 132
Columbia Records, 83
Communication
as basis of society, 36
Community service, 71, 73
Compression
AAC, 44–45
audio, 13, 38–39
video, 27, 40
Computers, personal
as force against corporations, 63

increased sales of, 108
media uniting with, 36
popularity increase of, 18
power of, 3
Rio player and, 59
as stereo, 29
Concerts
Riffage, 94
sponsorship of, 76–77, 125
Conroy, Kevin, 184
Constitution, 121
Consumer Electronic Association, 175
Consumers
Gracenote as music browser for, 182–183
interests of, 155–156
InterTrust, freedom and, 147
Napster benefit for, 116–117, 120
P2P for, 186
resistance to Napster court decision by, 180
rights of, 3
Content, 16
Cooney, Manus, 176
Copy protection, 44–45
digital recorder, 57
Copyright, 124
affirmation of, 174
audiocassettes and, 3
criminal statute and, 161
digital realm clarification of, 88
fair use of, 85
infringement of, 86, 120–121, 134, 142
injunctions and, 157–158
Internet threat of, 59
issues of, 113
lack of creativity, enforcement and, 68
lawsuit case of violation of, 143
lawyer's threat for, 24
licensing of, 120
Napster infringement of, 104, 142, 171–172
neutering of, 137
protection of, 121, 176

service *vs.* technology and, 159–160

Sony case, non-infringement use and, 158–159, 161, 175

unenforceability of, 118

use-it-or-lose-it, 86

violations of, 84

Copyright Act, 121

Cornyn, Stan, 26

Corporate mergers, 23

Costello, Elvis, 69

The Cranberries, 26

Creativity

stealing from others for, 68

Critics, 95–96

Curry, Steve, 145

DAT (digital audio tape), 3

Davis, Clive, 164, 167

Deadheads, 17–18

innovations from, 41

trading of tapes on Internet by, 19

Def Jam Records, 82

Demonstrators, 7–8

Dial-in computer networks, 18

Diamond, Mike, 65–66

Diamond Multimedia

lawsuit against Rio player of, 57–59

Diamond Rio, 88

Digibox secure containers, 147

Digital Automatic Music (DAM), 89

Digital distribution. *See* Online distribution

Digital Millennium Copyright Act (DMCA), 88, 113, 140, 156, 163, 175

Digital music

vinyl *vs.*, 183

Digital production studio, 34

Digital recorders

music industry royalty from manufactures of, 57

Digital signal processing, 13

Disintermediation, 132

Dolby, 44

Dolby, Ray, 41

Dole, Bob, 181

Domain name

name-recognition of, 48, 53

purchase of, 47–48

The Doors, 84

Dornemann, Michael, 167

"Downloadable music: Revolution or Revitalization," 51

Downloading

barrier eliminated for, 38–39

Dr. Dre, 114, 125, 128, 181

Napster *vs.*, 114–115

DSL, 108

Duran Duran, 45–46

Dylan, Bob, 83

"The Economy of Ideas" (Barlow), 20

Egreetings Network, 164

Electronic Frontier Foundation, 19, 38

Elektra Records, 84, 133

E-mail, 17

fans addresses of, 67

registration on, 45

EMI, 1, 23–24, 81–82, 96, 106

Liquid Audio and, 109, 149

online strategy (pay *vs.* free) of, 149–152

record companies and holdings under, 83

Eminem, 114–115, 117, 125, 128, 181

Emusic, 49, 58, 123, 145

Napster and, 104–105, 174

non-use of encryption by, 92

online subscription service of, 69, 145, 173

sales online for, 92–94

sells lacking in, 122

Encryption, 92–93,147

Engineers

record company *vs.*, 90

Eno, Brian, 74

Entertainment companies

consolidation of, 145

Epic Records, 83

Eritmo.com, 164

Eurythmics, 64

Fair use, 85
FanGlobe, 164
Fanning, John, 102–104, 124
Fanning, Shawn, 2, 10, 110, 132, 157,
    180. *See also* Napster
  childhood of, 101–103
  congressional hearing and, 162–163
  growing up of, 165
  Metallic lawsuit response by, 113
  Metallica and, 167–168
  re-tooling of Napster after court
    decision by, 177
Fanning Shawn, 132
Fans
  artists, technology and, 176
  e-mail addresses of, 67
  embittered online, 86
  group's international online, 72–73
  against Metallica, 114
  nurturing of, 66
  organizing community of, 71
  record company, web sites and, 109
  RIAA pressure on, 86–87
  Star Trek, 86
  threatened web sites of, 85
  Web sites and natural relationship
    with, 69–70
Farber, David, 38
Farrace, Mike, 51
Federal Trade Commission, 38
File Transfer Protocol (FTP), 14
Film, 82–83, 156–157
550 Music, 83
Flynn, Robert, 43
Foo Fighters, 108
4AD Records, 15
Frackman, Russell, 159–161
Frankel, Jeff, 97
Frankel, Justin, 2, 55–56, 132–133,
    147–148
Frauenhofer, 27, 53
Freenet, 134–137, 176, 178, 179
  P2P and, 186
Fripp, Robert, 152–153
FTP directories, 18
FTP sites, 29

Gabriel, Peter, 74
Garageband.com
  contests for unknown artists and,
    73–74
Garcia, Jerry, 18
Gassner, Rudi, 167
Geffen, David, 30
Geffen Records, 24, 27, 82, 90, 126
  concerns of, 30–31
GetMusic, 109, 164
Glaser, Rob, 35–36, 46, 54, 155–156
Gnucleus, 134
Gnutella, 2, 56, 145, 176, 178, 179
  AOL and, 146–148
  P2P and, 186
  RIAA vs, 133–134
  without central server, 132–133
Goldring, Fred, 75, 137
Goo Goo Dolls, 126
GoodNoise. *See* Emusic
Gore, Al, 11–12
Gorman, Derek, 85
Gracenote
  CD database and, 182
  as music browser, 182–183
Grateful Dead, 40–42, 111
  after Garcia's death, 19
  freedom of music of, 17–18
Great American Music Hall, 95
Green, Michael, 51
Griffin, Jim, 27–28, 30–31, 69, 89–90,
    105, 128, 145, 151, 179
Gruner+Jahr magazines, 83
Gutenberg press, 17

Hackers, 133
Hagar, Sammy, 44
Hagelslag, 134
Hansen, Jacobsen, Teller & Hoberman,
    75
Harrison, Jerry, 73
Harry Fox Agency, 25, 105
  MP3.com *vs.*, 121
Hatch, Orin, 140, 156, 162–163
Hatch, Orrin, 175–176, 181
Havas Press, 82

Heinlein, Robert, 131
Hertz, Ken, 52, 71–72, 125–126, 126
  deal making abilities of, 75–77
  InterTrust, consumers and, 147
  marketing and, 152
  support of Napster by, 117–118
  Uprizer and, 137
Hetfield, James, 114
High-bandwidth connection, 2
Hill, Faith, 84
Hoffman, Gene, 174
Holtzman, Steve, 43–44
HotWired, 36, 39
House of Pain, 29
Houston, Whitney, 165
Hummer Winbald, 168
Hummer Winblad, 43–44, 55, 124
Hyman, David, 182–183

Ice-T, 24, 64, 115, 125, 185
  MP3.com and, 122
Independent labels
  larger distributor purchasing of, 24
  online distribution and, 93
Indiana University, 111–112
Information
  free trading of, 1, 4, 135–137
Information superhighway, 12, 107
Information theory, 13
Injustice, 8
Institut Integreirte Schaltungen, 27
Integrated Media Systems, 42, 43
Intel
  P2P and, 186
Intellectual property
  corporate legal departments for, 20
  disregard of, 51–52
  giving away of, 18
  instantaneous distribution and, 20
  Napster protecting of, 134
  protection of, 138–140
  RIAA protection of, 176
  sharing of, 162
International
  online distribution, 72–73
International Federation of the
  Phonographic Industry (IFPI), 177

Internet, 1, 184. *See also* P2P; Online
  Distribution; Web sites
  AOL purchase of Time Warner and,
    84, 109, 145
  broadcasting over, 94
  community nature of, 155–156
  data constraints on, 78
  file sharing on, 16, 121, 124,
    135–136, 141, 163, 166, 168
  growth of, 15
  high-bandwidth connection on, 2
  infancy of, 2
  information superhighway of, 12, 107
  as laboratory for musicians, 64
  major labels hesitancy about, 26–27
  as marketing tool, 66
  music listeners on, 61
  myth of power of, 107–108
  newspapers on, 28, 185
  not immune to copyright, 143
  original goals of, 16
  radio, 97–98
  revival of career through, 64
  RIAA threatened by, 58–59
  self-marketing on, 44
  sharing information on, 16
  simultaneous streaming f, 95
  slower connections on, 35, 38
  song released in stores and on, 45–46
Internet company
  irrational exuberance of, 93–94
Internet Relay Chat (IRC), 102
Internet Service Provider (ISP), 158
Internet Underground Music Archive
  (IUMA), 14–16, 29, 40, 55
  closing of, 174
  unsigned artists, Internet and, 14–16,
    51
Interscope, 82, 117
InterTrust, 139
  AOL and, 146–147
  BMG and, 146
  Universal and, 146
Investors, 122. *See also* Venture capital
IPO, 40
  Artist Direct, 123
  MP3.com, 71–72, 76–79, 103

Island Records, 82
ISO-MPEG Audio Layer–3. *See* MP3
IUMA. *See* Internet Underground
    Music Archive

J Records, 164
Jackson, Michael, 62–63
Jagged Little Pill, 75
Jive Records, 117
John, Elton, 5

Kan, Gene, 134, 177, 179–180
Kapor, Mitch, 38
Kearby, Gerry, 41–46, 50, 79
    for musician's rights and ownership,
        54–55
Kesey, Ken, 40
King, Howard, 9, 111, 112, 114, 115,
        117, 167
King Crimson, 152–153
Klein, Joel, 185
Knitting Factory, 95
Kohn, Bob, 92
Kohn, Robert, 58
Kraftwerk, 70
Kravitz, Lenny, 83

La Junta, 70
    MP3.com and, 71–73
Law. *See also* Intellectual property
Lawsuit(s), 3. *See also* Legal threats
    BMG *vs.* 'N Sync, 167
    copyright, 10
    Diamond Multimedia *vs.* RIAA,
        57–59
    Metallica *vs.* Napster, 111–115, 167
    Metallica *vs.* Universities, 111–112,
        132
    MP3.com *vs.* Harry Fox Agency, 121
    MP3.com vs. RIAA, 119–122
    MP3.com *vs.* TVT Records, 121
    MP3.com *vs.* Universal Music
        Group, 140, 143
    Napster and, 99
    online distribution, web sites and,
        88
    RIAA *vs.* Napster, 118, 141–142, 155

RIAA *vs.* Napster (in Ninth Circuit
    Court of Appeals), 142–143,
    157–162, 171–172
Sony video recorder, 141, 158
Lawyers, 8, 11, 24, 52, 71–72, 92, 124,
    140–141, 157–159
    lobbying by, 87
    value of, 75–76
Led Zeppelin, 84
Legal threats, 156
    against OLGA, 106
    against Web sites, 86–87
Leonard, Hal, 106
Lessig, Lawrence, 180
Lew, Brian, 113
Licensing, 140 (find more)
Lillywhite, Steve, 74
Limp Bizkit, 125
Liquid Audio, 40–41, 92, 108, 109, 123,
    124
    Capitol and, 45–46
    EMI and, 149
    future of, 181–182
    like railway for Internet, 54
    MP3 format added to, 55
    MP3 *vs.*, 54
    N2K and, 55–56
    security features of, 44–45, 50–51
    special format of, 46
    stock growth of, 78–79
    threefold aspect of, 44–45
Listen.com, 164
    invest by major labels in, 96
    as music portal, 95–96
Lopez, Jennifer, 83
Lord, Rob, 12–16, 27, 29, 30, 55, 97,
    113, 145–146, 167, 168, 183
Love, Courtney, 5, 52, 137
    against record company, 125–128
LP. *See* Albums

Maxell, 134
Madonna, 70, 76–77
mailing lists
    Grateful Dead, 17
Major labels
    corporate mergers and, 23

friendships among, 184
revenue of, 23
Marketing
heavy-handed, 12
online street, 71
online *vs.* standard, 152
The Marshall Mathers LP, 114
Martin, Sir George, 74
Maverick Records, 76–77, 96
MCA Nashville Records, 82
MCA records, 75
McCartney, Paul, 121
McGuinn, Roger, 64
MCM Records, 82
Meat Loaf, 68
Mechanical rights, 25
Media, 145
as basis of society, 36
hyper, 38
Media Minds, 47
Mercury Records, 82
Messier, Jean-Marie, 178, 184
Metallica, 181
concert *vs.* studio music by, 111
fans of, 111
Napster and, 110, 167–168
Napster *vs.*, 4, 7–10, 111–115, 167
original tape-trading network of, 113
ripped off feeling of, 64–65
Microsoft, 36–38, 158, 181, 185
P2P and, 124
Midbar, 110
Middlehoff, Thomas, 5, 116, 163–164,
    166–167, 171, 179, 184
Middlemen, 131–132
Mjuice, 105, 108
sells lacking in, 122
Modems
14.4 kbs, 35
faster, 40
slower, 38
Modern Lover, 73
Monovox, 74
Morissette, Alanis, 52, 143
background of, 74–75
MP3.com and, 76–79
tour sponsorship for, 76–77

Mosaic, 13, 28, 36
Motion Picture Association of America,
    156
Motion Picture Experts Group, 91
Moving Pixels, 137
MP2
algorithm, 13
MP3, 2, 3, 18, 27, 29
AAC *vs.*, 44–45
after Napster decision, 175
brainstorming with, 50
connection through, 186
encryption and, 92–93
flexible updates through, 34
free, 29
free music, not free for musicians
    and, 54
graphic user interface for, 56
illegal copying and, 91–92
lack of security in, 50
Liquid Audio *vs.*, 54
listening ease of, 96
live recordings from, 66–67
Motion Picture Experts Group and,
    91
music sharing by, 110
musicians use of, 67
opening of music by, 74
player, 40, 63, 96, 182
potential of, 30
protocols of, 13
recognition of, 78
Rio player and, 59
sampling value of, 128
single, 124
stereo quality player, 55
summit, 48–49, 75, 78, 137
technology of, 86–87
tidal wave of, 46
Walkman-like devices for, 57
MP3 Audio Consortium (M3C), 47
MP3.com, 31, 35, 46–55
access to already owned CD via, 119
advertising revenue for, 54
Alanis Morissette and, 76–79, 144
Beam-It from, 119–122
Beastie Boys and, 67

building of brand recognition by, 50,
52–53, 78
Harry Fox Agency *vs.*, 121
Ice-T and, 72, 122
IPO of, 71–72, 76–78, 103
La Junta, 71–73
lawsuit against, 118
legal representation of, 75
lumped with Napster, 144
major record companies ignored
areas and, 88–89
musicians and, 46–47
against Napster, 118
online subscription service of, 69
opening day of IPO of, 78–79
options from, 77, 92
Payback for Playback by, 144–145
radical music models by, 144
RIAA *vs.*, 119–122
settlement of Beam-It judgement
against, 122
settlements with record companies
by, 143, 181
subscription models for, 145, 173
TVT Records *vs.*, 121
uncivilized approach of, 139
Universal Music Group *vs.*, 140, 143
MPL Communication, 121
MR Mac, 47
MTV, 10, 62
Internet released video before, 66
Music
change in ways of listening to, 58
digital, 70–71
free, 135–137, 184
intricacy of, 33
sharing of, 141
simultaneous streaming of, 95
ubiquity of, 151–152
Music distribution. *See* Record
distribution
The Music Group, 26–27
Music industry. *See also* Record
companies
big-record-label-dominated, 2
control by, 1
demise of, 14

digital recorder manufactures royalty
to, 57
jumping ship from, 89
legal skirmishes of, 3
as middlemen, 131–132
percentage sale of all blank tapes for,
3
recession for, 62
Secure Digital Music Initiative and,
90–91
slowness of, 90
software piracy protection as model
for, 52
Musicians. *See also* Artists
deals for, xvi
ear listening/copying by, 105–106
promoting popularity of, 106
web sites of, 65–66
MusicMarc, 118
MusicMatch, 49, 96
MyGnut, 134
Myhrvold, Nathan, 36

'N Sync, 117, 167
Name
as valuable, 77, 89, 128–129
Navigator, 134
Napster, 40, 55, 92, 110
appeal and Ninth Circuit decision
for, 142–143, 157–162, 171–172
artist against, 125, 128
artist for, 125–126
artist respect by, 10
availability of music on, 108
Bertelsmann's investment in, 5,
163–165, 167, 171
Bertelsmann, security and, 165
colleges and, 109, 111–112
commercial music shared in, 104
community of, 186
consumer benefit by, 116–117, 120
corporate-sanctioned model of,
169–170
demonstrators at, 7–8
Digital Millennium Copyright Act
(DMCA) used by, 113
disappointment in appeal at, 175

Dr. Dre *vs.*, 114–115
ease of use of, 108
Emusic and, 104–105
expelling anyone infringing copyright
    by, 113
as "fair use" of music, 160
Fanning's speech to congressional
    hearing for, 162–163
free speech and, 112
Hatch's adviser hired by, 176
help artist success by, 117
imitators of, 2, 132, 134, 176
lawsuit ruling against, 141–142
lawsuits and, 99
lawyer for, 140–141
legal defense by, 141–142
limited effect on record sales by, 152
limited injunction after appeal for,
    171–172
management of, 124
Metallica *vs.*, 4, 7–10, 110–115, 167
millions of users of, 156, 157, 166,
    170, 175
monthly fee of, 171
movies, pornography, software
    through, 123–124
MP3.com *vs.*, 118, 120
music in people's lives and, 153
no admission of guilt by, 165
non-American users of, 173
police raids of international users of,
    177
post court decision, changing nature
    of, 177–178
P2P and, 103, 185–186
price *vs.* piracy and, 129
profit potential for, 115–116
protocol of, 112
record companies waiting for
    settlement with, 178
record promotion through, 117–118
RIAA *vs.*, 104, 118, 141–142, 155
self-protecting of, 134
service *vs.* technology nature of,
    159–160
sharing, linking source of, 103
shutting of, xvi

Ted Cohen consultant to, 151
theft of music by, 8
uncertainty of royalties and, 172–173
uncivilized approach of, 139
Universal Music Group *vs.*, 140
Weekly workarounds for, 112
Wrapster of, 123–124
writing beginning program for, 103
National Center for Supercomputing
    Applications, 13
National Music Publishers' Association,
    25
National Music Publishers' Association
    (NMPA), 106
Net. *See* Internet
NetGames, 102
NetPD, 10
New product, 3
New York Dolls, 68
Newspapers, 185
N2K, 45, 57
    Liquid Audio and, 55–56
Nogueras, Jose "Gridlock," 70
Nogueras, Xavier "X-Man," 70–73
Nonprofit status
    educational tools and, 106
North by Northwest, 94
Nullsoft, 56–57, 145. *See also* Winamp
    AOL and, 97–98, 148–149
    Gnutella on web site of, 132–134
    InterTrust encryption sell out and, 147

Oasis, 70
    fan web sites of, 85
    legal threat by, 85
Oasis Webmasters for Internet
    Freedom, 85
OLGA (On Line Guitar Archive)–106,
    105
Online distribution. *See also* Record
    promotion
    artist recognition on, 128–129
    artists payment from, 144–145
    beginning of, 11
    CDNow, 109
    copyright infringement and, 134–135
    digital production studio and, 34

EMI, 149–152
Emusic, 92–94, 145, 174
encryption and, 92
format for sales on, 92–94
free domain of, 15
GetMusic, 109
independent labels use of, 93
infancy of, 28–29
international, 72–73
investor withdrawal from, 122
legitimate, 88, 92
Liquid Audio, 109
Listen.com as music portal and,
    95–96
low cost of, 34–35
major labels and, 96
Napster affect on, 104–105
N2K, 55–56
promotion of unknown group
    through, 70
promotion through, 28
radical Internet use by, 35
reps of, 8
record company's technology
    problems with, 178–179
RIAA pressuring of, 81–82, 84
Riffage, 94–95
song released in stores and on,
    45–46
street marketing of, 71
Sony subscription service of, 139
subscription model for, 69, 105, 173,
    178
unknown artists use of, 14–16, 51,
    73–74, 94–95
Online music, 15
  advancement of, 98
  evangelist, 14
  MP3.com brand recognition in, 50,
    52–53
Online music retailer. *See also* Online
    distribution
  concerns of, 45
  N2K, 55–56
Open Nap, 134
Options, 77, 92, 123
O'Reilly, 179–180

Parker, Sean, 103
Parres, John, 48–49
Patel, Judge, 141–143
PatroNet, 68
Patterson, Jeff, 12–16, 27, 97, 174
PayLars.com, 114
Peer International, 121
Penalties
  MP3.com lawsuit, 143
Pepper, Tom, 56, 148
Percolator, 134
Petty, Tom, 123
Philips, 26, 110
  CD development by, 62
Piracy
  RIAA as watchdog for, 81, 84–85
Pittman, Bob, 62, 97
Player technology, 13
Polygram, 82
PopKomm, 116
Pornster, 134
Powell, Adam, 134
P2P (peer-to-peer), 124, 133, 136, 141,
    163, 179–180, 185
Pretty Good Privacy, 92
Programmer
  power of, 2
Progressive Networks, 38
Project Zeus, 165
Promoters
  independent, 24
Promotion. See also Online
    Distribution; Record promotion
  Internet, 28
Psychoacoustic models, 27
Public Enemy, 10
Public injury, 172

Racketeering Influenced and Corrupt
    Organizations Act, 111
Radio, 97–98
  interactive, 118
  Internet distribution by, 39–40
  record company coagulation with, 117
Radiohead, 4
Rakoff, Jed, 120–121, 143
Random House, 83

Rave scene, 12
RCA Records, 82
Reagan, Ronald, 11
Real Conference, 138
RealAudio, 35–37. *See also*
    RealNetworks
  audio compression by, 38–39
  radio station's Net distribution and,
    39–40
RealNetworks, 40, 46, 54, 155
  future of, 181
  Real Entertainment Center of, 96
  RealJukebox by, 40, 96, 182
  Universal and, 138–139
  video compression by, 40
Record companies *See also* Independent
    labels; Lawsuits; Major labels
  artists, renegotiation of contract and,
    151
  artists against, 52, 59, 126–127
  avoidance of downloading by, 39
  business model of, xv-xvi
  copy protection for, 44–45
  costs for, 4
  customers *vs.* purchasers issue for,
    179
  downloadable music seminar and, 51
  downloaders, uploaders and, 161
  engineers *vs.*, 90
  fan websites and, 109
  against free Internet music, 51–52
  independence among major, 81–82, 84
  lost of control, MTV and, 62–63
  major vs. independent, 23
  MP3 conference and, 49–50
  MP3.com settlements with, 181
  Napster, growth of CD sales and,
    152, 165
  non-American customers of, 173
  online distribution technology
    problems with, 178–179
  online distributor and, 109
  online subscription service of, 69
  preserving of status quo by, 155–156
  radio coagulation with, 117
  recognition of cool idea of Napster
    by, 116–117

  RIAA as voice for, 81–82, 84
  Virtual world *vs.* real world for, 147
  waiting for Napster settlement by,
    178
Record distribution, 12
  new methods of, 3
Record labels. *See* Record company
Record promotion. *See also* Online
    Distribution
  artist recognition and online,
    128–129
  difficulty of breaking record through,
    117–118
  EMI poor online, 149
  high costs of, 4, 69, 117–118
  legal opinion on file sharing, 121
  name recognition of, 89
  Napster as, 117–118
  radio, 117
  word of mouth, 118
Recording
  live performance, 18
Recording Academy
  downloadable music seminar and,
    51–52
Recording contract
  winning online of, 73
Recording Industry Association of
    America. *See* RIAA
Recording studio, 33–34
Red Hot Chili Peppers, 84
Reid, Robert, 95
Relativity Records, 83
Reno vs. ACLU, 180
Reprise Records, 84
Retailers
  EMI, online distribution and,
    149–150
  nervousness of, 44–45
  trouble making money by, 117
Rhymes, Busta, 125, 128
RIAA, xvi, 4, 8, 48, 52
  activities of, 24
  appeal by Napster against, 142–143
  Artists Against Piracy funding by, 125
  artists grievances against, 126
  artists investment concern of, 162

expanding the image of, 181
fan Web sites pressured/closed by, 86–87
Gnutella *vs.*, 133–134
increasing power of, 173
intellectual property and, 176
lawsuit against Diamond Multimedia by, 57–59
lawsuit threats by, 156
legitimate online distribution desired by, 88, 92
licensing issues for, 140
MP3.com *vs.*, 119–122
Napster, Bertelsmann and, 168
Napster (in Ninth Circuit Court of Appeals) *vs.*, 142–143, 157–162, 171–172
Napster *vs.*, 104, 118, 141–142, 155
online companies pressured by, 81–82
rethinking Internet by, 99–100
role of, 81, 152–153
Secure Digital Music Initiative (SDMI) and, 59, 90, 109
Ted Cohen consultant to, 151
Richards, Keith, 63
Richardson, Eileen, 124
Riffage, 164
unknown artists distribution by, 94–95
Rights. *See also* Copyright
difficulty in maintaining of, 68
digital management of, 147
exclusive, 48, 121
holders of, 54
infringement of, 3
mechanical, 25
piracy of, 84
as valuable, 77
Rio player
lawsuit against, 57
Ritter, John, 103
Robertson, Michael, 31, 46–55, 58, 103. *See also* MP3.com
Alanis Morissette and, 76–77
Beastie Boys and, 67
building of one-man brand by, 50, 52–53

as de facto spokesman, 53
IPO and, 78–79
La Junta and, 71
major record companies ignored areas and, 88–89
MP3.com radical music approach by, 144
Napster and, 118, 120
settlement of Beam-It judgement against, 122
Universal penalty and, 143
Rogers, Ian, 30, 56, 65–67, 145
Rolling Stones, 63, 70
Rosen, Hilary, 57, 99–100, 140, 156
Internet infringement fight by, 87–88
MP3.com litigation and, 119–120
Napster lawsuit and, 118, 161–162, 167–168, 173–174
Royalties, 25
Rundgren, Todd, 145
copyright issues and, 68
fans and, 69–70
PatroNet of, 68

Sammit, Jay, 149
San Franciso Bay, 40–41
San Mateo, California, 5
Santa Cruz, California, 11
Santana, 165
scarcity, 35
Schmidt, Andreas, 164, 178
SEC regulations, 123
Secure Digital Music Initiative (SDMI), 90–91
SESAC (Society of European Stage Authors and Composers), 25
Shaw, Anthony, 74
Sheet Music Direct, 106
Sinatra, Frank, 84
Singers
deals for, xvi
Slash.dot.org, 115
Smashing Pumpkins
free distribution on Net by, 4
Smith, Patti, 68
Smith, Will, 52
Sniping, 71

Social activism, 19–20, 36–37, 112, 135, 144, 180
Software
  flexible updates through, 34
  open-source movement of, 115
  piracy protection by, 52
  speed of duplication from, 3–4
Software Development Forum, 43
Songbooks, 105–106
Songwriters. *See also* Artists
  deals for, xvi
  royalties for, 25
Sonique, 96
Sony Music, 1, 109, 110, 167
  CD development by, 62
  Oasis, legal threat and, 85
  record companies and holdings under, 83
  subscription service of, 139
  video recorder lawsuit against, 141, 158
Sony vs. Universal City Studio, 158
South by Southwest, 94
Spears, Britney, 117
Spinner, 97, 184
Springsteen, Bruce, 83
Spyster, 134
Stanford Artificial Intelligence Lab, 17
Stanford University, 28–30, 40–41, 124, 180
  free speech and, 112
Star Trek, 86
Steadman, Carl, 95
Stewart, Dave, 64
Sting, 26
Stone, Noah, 125
Streisand, Barbra, 83
Suck.com, 95
Supposed Former Infatuation Junkie, 76
Supreme Court, 158, 175, 180
Swap meets, 160
Synthesizer, 34

Talking Heads, 73
TCP/IP, 37

Technology, 70–71
  copyright and, 158–159, 175
  power of, 2–3
Television, 82–83, 94
  interactive, 38
Theft
  cool, 116
  electronic, 116
They Might Be Giants, 93, 174
Thought-leader, 28
Thriller, 62–63
Titanic, 138
Tour. *See*
Tower Records, 51, 149
Townshend, Peter, 5
Transworld, 149
Tri-Star Music, 83
TVT Records
  MP3.com *vs.*, 121

Ulrich, Lars, 4, 8–10, 108, 114, 115, 125, 126, 162, 167–168
Ultimate Band List, 95
Ultrasound, 41
Universal, 1, 23–24, 28
Universal Classics Group, 82
Universal Motown Records Group, 82
Universal Music Group, 51–52, 78, 90, 96. *See also* Vivendi Universal
  GetMusic and, 109
  Internet strategy of, 139–140
  InterTrust and, 146
  MP3.com *vs.*, 140, 143
  Napster and, 167
  Napster *vs.*, 124–125, 140
  RealNetworks and, 138–139
  record companies and holdings under, 82
Universal Pictures, 82
Universal Studios, 82
Universities, 111–112, 132
Uprizer, 118
U.S. Advanced Research Projects Agency (ARPA), 16

Usenet, 105
Utopia, 16–17

Vanilla Ice, 75
Venture capital, 43–44, 124, 156. *See also* Investors
Verve Pipe, 29
Verve Records, 82
    Internet released, 66
Video compression, 27, 40
Videos, music
    as advertising, 62–63
    costs for, 63
    Internet released, 66
Virgin Records, 24, 81, 83, 149
    Smashing Pumpkins broke with, 4
Virtual world
    real world *vs.*, 147
Vivendi Universal, 82, 178
    other labels and, 184–185
    setting up for Net-centric future by, 181
    Universal purchased by, 138

Waits, Tom, 23, 93
Walt Disney
    Artists Against Piracy funding by, 125
"Walter's War," 82
Warner American Express Satellite Entertainment Company (WASEC), 62
Warner Brothers, 1, 13, 23–24, 25–26, 82, 84, 126, 133. *See also* AOL Time Warner
4AD Records of, 15
Washingtonpost.com, 185
Watermark, 44–45
    CD, 93
    CD's without, 62, 109–110

Waters, Muddy, 63
Web. *See* Internet
Web sites
    fan nurturing on, 66–67, 69, 71–72
    group's international, 72–73
    MP3.com making of band's, 48
    musician's, 15, 48, 65–66
    Nullsoft, 133
    RIAA pressuring/closing of, 86–87
    threatened fan, 85–86
Webnoize, 68
Weekly, David, 28–30, 47, 48, 49, 77, 86, 90
    Napster workarounds by, 112
Welch, Scott, 76–77
WELL, 18
Wherehouse, 149
The Who, 5
Whole Earth Catalog, 18
Winamp, 40, 56–57, 96, 145, 184
    new version of, 147
    non-corporate nature of, 147
    record companies and, 50
Winbald, Ann, 43–44
Wired, 12
Wirt, Ken, 94–95
Wiser, Phil, 43
Work-for-hire, 126, 170, 174
Wrapster, 123–124

Xing Player, 13, 50

Yahoo, 10
Yaunch, Adam, 65–66
Yetznikoff, Walter, 82
Y2K, 107

Zelnick, Straus, 167